The Amazing Adventures of
MR. GRANT MONEY

Dear Reader,

Thank you for joining us on this exciting journey with The Amazing Adventures of Mr. Grant Money. I'm thrilled to share the valuable insights and transformative lessons within these pages —lessons that have empowered countless students, educators, and organizations to achieve remarkable success in securing scholarships and grant funding.

Scholarships and grants are powerful tools for opening doors to opportunity, and this book is designed to be your trusted companion as you navigate the intricate world of funding for education. Within these stories, you'll find not just engaging narratives but essential lessons and strategies to guide you and your students toward securing the financial support needed to achieve your academic goals.

This book is more than a collection of stories—it's part of a comprehensive approach to scholarship and grant education. As you read and engage with the exercises, I hope you discover actionable strategies and inspiration to elevate your efforts to new heights.

I'd also like to introduce you to an invaluable resource: our specially curated content on the Mr. Grant Money website. At www.mrgrantmoney.com/college-scholarships, you'll find in-depth information, book reviews, bonus content, and resources to help you go even further. This is just one book in a five-part series, each designed as part of a comprehensive curriculum that can guide you and your students through an entire year of training in grant and scholarship acquisition.

When you visit our website, be sure to check out the blog, where you'll find additional stories and articles. You'll also enjoy our deep-dive interviews and podcast-style discussions that make learning both enjoyable and engaging. For schools and organizations interested in maximizing the impact of this curriculum, I encourage you to explore our licensing program, which provides access to exclusive resources, saves time, and helps you make the most of these lessons.

Finally, because we believe learning should be both fun and memorable, don't miss the Mr. Grant Money music collection—a perfect complement to this educational journey. With its upbeat tracks and inspirational messages, the music is a great way to enhance the learning experience for you and your students. Explore more at www.mrgrantmoney.com/music.
Thank you for allowing The Amazing Adventures of Mr. Grant Money to be a part of your educational journey. Together, let's unlock the doors to opportunity and success!

Best Regards,

Rodney

Grant Central USA

P.S. Be sure to visit our website and sign up for our newsletters to stay current.

The Amazing Adventures of

MR. GRANT MONEY

Empowering Futures: Scholarships With Lasting Impact

VOLUME FIVE

RODNEY WALKER

Chief Editor: Laine Minerales
Editorial Assistant: Daniel Tuano
Production Supervisor: Joerje Galo
Electronic Composition: Jairus Agoncillo
Photographer: Studio 5404
Executive Marketing Manager: Jimmy Moore

Discover the breadth of our series, encompassing a myriad of crucial topics. Delve into the realms of grant acquisition, college scholarships, entrepreneurship, social impact, philanthropy, and beyond. Unearth a treasure trove of knowledge and empowerment within our diverse collection. Explore the wealth of insights awaiting you across these transformative series.

To inquire about utilizing The Amazing Adventures of Mr. Grant Money books in the classroom, securing licensing, and exploring special pricing for bulk orders, kindly contact us at info@grantcentralusa.com.

ISBN: 979-8-89725-036-3 (Hardback)
ISBN: 979-8-89725-004-2 (Paperback)
ISBN: 979-8-89725-037-0 (Ebook)
ISBN: 979-8-89725-042-4 (Audiobook)

Printed in the United States

Dedication

This book is for the unstoppable—the ones who rise every time they fall and use every setback as fuel for their comeback. To those who've faced challenges head-on and emerged stronger, wiser, and ready for more. You are living proof that greatness isn't about never falling; it's about always getting back up. Your perseverance is inspiring, and your future is limitless. Keep reaching for the stars—I'm here cheering for your success.

With love and appreciation,
Rodney

PREFACE

I will never forget the day I walked into my high school guidance counselor's office, eager to embrace the challenge of honors English. The summer had been spent in a relentless pursuit of knowledge, and I believed I was ready to take on the academic challenges that awaited me. Little did I know that this simple request would set the stage for a pivotal moment that would shape my trajectory through my senior year and beyond.

My counselor, perhaps fueled by a misguided notion, walked me down the hallway and gestured towards a nearly all-white honors English classroom. With a pointed question, she challenged my ability to compete with the students within. In that moment, my confidence wavered, and the doubt crept in. As a senior in my final year of high school, the seed of uncertainty took root. If my counselor questioned my readiness, maybe I wasn't up to the challenge.

Regrettably, I succumbed to that doubt and chose not to enroll in honors English. It marked the beginning of a phase where I stopped giving my best and started coasting through the remainder of my senior year, doing just enough to get by. Little did I realize the impact this decision would have on my direct path to the college of my choice. While I did eventually find my way to that desired college, the journey was not straightforward. I was uninformed about the college application process, and the entire endeavor felt like a maze with no guide to lead me through. I vividly remember the moment of embarrassment when a peer proudly announced her chosen college, and I found myself unable to answer the same question because I hadn't even applied.

It was this moment of realization, coupled with my own winding journey to college and later earning a Master's in Business Administration, that fueled a promise to myself. I vowed that when the time was right, I would do my part to help others navigate the complex terrain of college admissions and secure scholarships for a brighter future.

This book is the fulfillment of that promise.

While there are countless books on scholarships and navigating the college landscape, I wanted to offer something different. Inspired by my own experiences, I sought to create a book that not only imparts practical knowledge but also inspires young readers to dream bigger. I want to encourage them with stories that stretch the imagination and showcase the boundless possibilities that education and perseverance can unlock.

As I reflect on that fateful day in the hallway, where uncertainty and embarrassment loomed large, I am grateful for the counselor whose words became the catalyst for this journey. In many ways, her doubts became the fuel that propelled me to excel, and now, with this book, I am committed to providing the guidance and inspiration I wish I had received.

To every young mind yearning for knowledge, every dreamer aspiring to greatness, and every individual navigating the intricate path to higher education, may this book be a beacon of hope and a source of invaluable scholarship success secrets.

With determination and dedication,

Rodney Walker

TABLE OF CONTENT

INTRODUCTION

Have you ever imagined scholarships as not just pathways to education but as tools to create a lasting impact? As we embark on the fifth volume of "The Amazing Adventures of Mr. Grant Money," get ready to delve into an immersive journey of scholarships with enduring significance.

In a world where education paves the way for the future, the significance of scholarships reaches far beyond financial aid. The adventures awaiting you within these pages transcend the ordinary, promising not just academic guidance but a profound understanding of how scholarships can empower futures.

This volume is a testament to the transformative power of scholarships, strategically woven into ten engaging stories that will captivate your imagination and reshape your perspective. Get ready for an exploration that goes beyond the conventional, offering a unique lens through which to view the impact of education.

Prepare to be immersed in a tapestry of scholarship tales, painted with vivid strokes that bring each adventure to life. This isn't just a guide; it's a sensory experience, where the impact of scholarships resonates in every word and every narrative twist.

As we unfold the pages of "Empowering Futures," the tone is one of inspiration and discovery. It's a journey infused with the optimism of scholarships and the belief that education can create ripples of lasting impact. Let the tone resonate with the optimism that each scholarship adventure holds.

Enter the world of scholarships guided by the ever-inspiring Mr. Grant Money. His adventures will take you to the heart of impactful scholarships, introducing you to characters whose lives are transformed by the opportunities education provides.

Amidst the joy of scholarships, there lies a tension—the tension between potential and opportunity, dreams and reality. Uncover the conflicts that propel the narratives forward, leaving you eager to explore how each scholarship story unfolds.

The enigma lies in the impact of scholarships, an intrigue that will keep you turning pages, eager to uncover the profound effects education can have on individuals and communities.

This is not your ordinary guide. It's a concise exploration, offering a taste of the transformative power of scholarships without overwhelming you with details. Each story is a snapshot, inviting you to delve deeper into the broader narrative.

As we transition from this introduction into the main narrative, consider this a door opening to a world where scholarships aren't just financial aids but catalysts for lasting impact. The adventures of Mr. Grant Money await, promising an exploration that transcends the ordinary and reshapes your understanding of the profound influence scholarships can have. Get ready for a journey where learning is not just educational but empowering. The odyssey begins now.

SCHOLARLY WAVES

The Amazing Adventures of MR GRANT MONEY

Scholarly Waves: Mr. Grant Money's Ocean of Inspiration

Aboard The Ship Of Purpose, Learn The Art Of Creating Ripples Through Scholarship Success

As Mr. Grant Money stepped onto the luxurious cruise ship docked in Rio de Janeiro, Brazil, a radiant smile adorned his face. The sun hung low in the sky, casting warm hues over the bustling port. He took a deep breath of the salty air and declared, "Today is a great day to make a great day!" This catchphrase, a mantra he lived by, resonated with the infectious positivity that surrounded him.

Having just spent two weeks exploring the vibrant city, Mr. Grant Money, dapperly dressed in a tailored suit, drew the attention of onlookers. Whispers of curiosity echoed through the crowd, "Who is this man?" "What does he do?" The air buzzed with anticipation.

As he made his way to board the ship, a few young people and families recognized him. "Look, it's Mr. Grant Money! I've read his books and watched him on YouTube!" they exclaimed, eager to catch a glimpse of the man whose name was synonymous with scholarship success.

Onboard, Mr. Grant Money was given a special acknowledgment by the captain, who recognized him and implored him to share a few words with the passengers. Ever gracious, Mr. Grant Money accepted the invitation, turning this unexpected opportunity into a chance to inspire.

"Good day, fellow adventurers!" he began, his voice carrying a magnetic energy. "We are scholars on a ship, sailing high in purpose, embarking on a great adventure to become the very best versions of ourselves and make valuable contributions to the world."

He continued to share the origins of the word "scholarship" but painted a vivid picture of scholars on a ship, bound for greatness. The acronym S.H.I.P took on a new meaning — "Sailing High In Purpose." His words resonated deeply with the audience, each syllable carving a path to their hearts and minds.

"People, just like ships, leave a wake. Every scholarship is a chance to create ripples of positive change. I want you to think of scholarships as opportunities to sail high in purpose, leaving a wake of inspiration for others to follow."

With a nostalgic twinkle in his eye, Mr. Grant Money shared a personal story from his childhood. He spoke of skipping rocks on the water, each skip creating a ripple effect. "I wanted to cause more ripples," he confessed. "And that's what I encourage each of you to do. Continue the ripples, inspire others, and make a difference in the world."

His heartfelt speech moved the audience, capturing their attention and even coaxing a few tears. As he concluded, recalling the scholarship that had transformed his life, he clutched his Shirley Scepter and Golden Journal. In a moment of profound reflection, he jotted down a powerful quote: "Scholarship is the wind in our sails, propelling us to create ripples that touch the shores of greatness."

With a final nod, Mr. Grant Money gracefully moved on, leaving behind a wake of inspired minds ready to embark on their own journeys, sailing high in purpose, and creating ripples that would echo for generations to come.

"Today is not just a date; it's a destiny waiting to unfold. Embrace it, sail high in purpose, and leave a wake that echoes with the ripples of your greatness!"

- Mr. Grant Money

Exercise: "Create Your Scholarship S.H.I.P Manifesto"

Materials Needed:
- Large sheets of paper or poster boards
- Markers, pens, and other creative tools
- Stickers, glitter, or any other decorative items (optional)

Instructions:

1. Introduction (5 minutes):
- Gather the participants in a comfortable and creative space.
- Briefly share the story of Mr. Grant Money's cruise adventure, emphasizing the key themes of scholarships, purpose, and creating positive ripples.

2. Inspiration Session (10 minutes):
- Play a short video clip or read an excerpt from the story that highlights Mr. Grant Money's impromptu speech about scholarships and the S.H.I.P acronym.
- Ask participants to reflect on the key messages: sailing high in purpose, creating ripples, and the transformative power of scholarships.

3. Group Brainstorm (15 minutes):
- Divide participants into small groups (3-5 people per group).
- Provide each group with large sheets of paper or poster boards and a variety of creative tools.
- Instruct each group to brainstorm and create their own "Scholarship S.H.I.P Manifesto." Encourage them to include key elements like purpose, inspiration, and the idea of creating positive ripples.
- Participants can use drawings, words, and any other creative elements they feel represent their interpretation of the scholarship journey.

4. Manifesto Presentation (15 minutes):
- After the brainstorming session, each group presents their manifesto to the entire group.
- Encourage participants to explain the symbolism behind their choices and how their manifesto reflects the values and messages from Mr. Grant Money's story.

5. Gallery Walk and Reflection (10 minutes):
- Arrange the created manifestos around the room for a gallery walk.
- Participants walk around, observing and reflecting on the unique ideas and creativity expressed in each manifesto.
- After the walk, gather everyone for a brief reflection session. Ask participants to share their thoughts, key takeaways, and any personal connections they made during the activity.

This kickoff exercise not only sets a positive and creative atmosphere but also allows participants to express their interpretation of the story's themes in a visual and collaborative way. It's a fun and engaging way to start a storytelling session focused on scholarship impact and purpose.

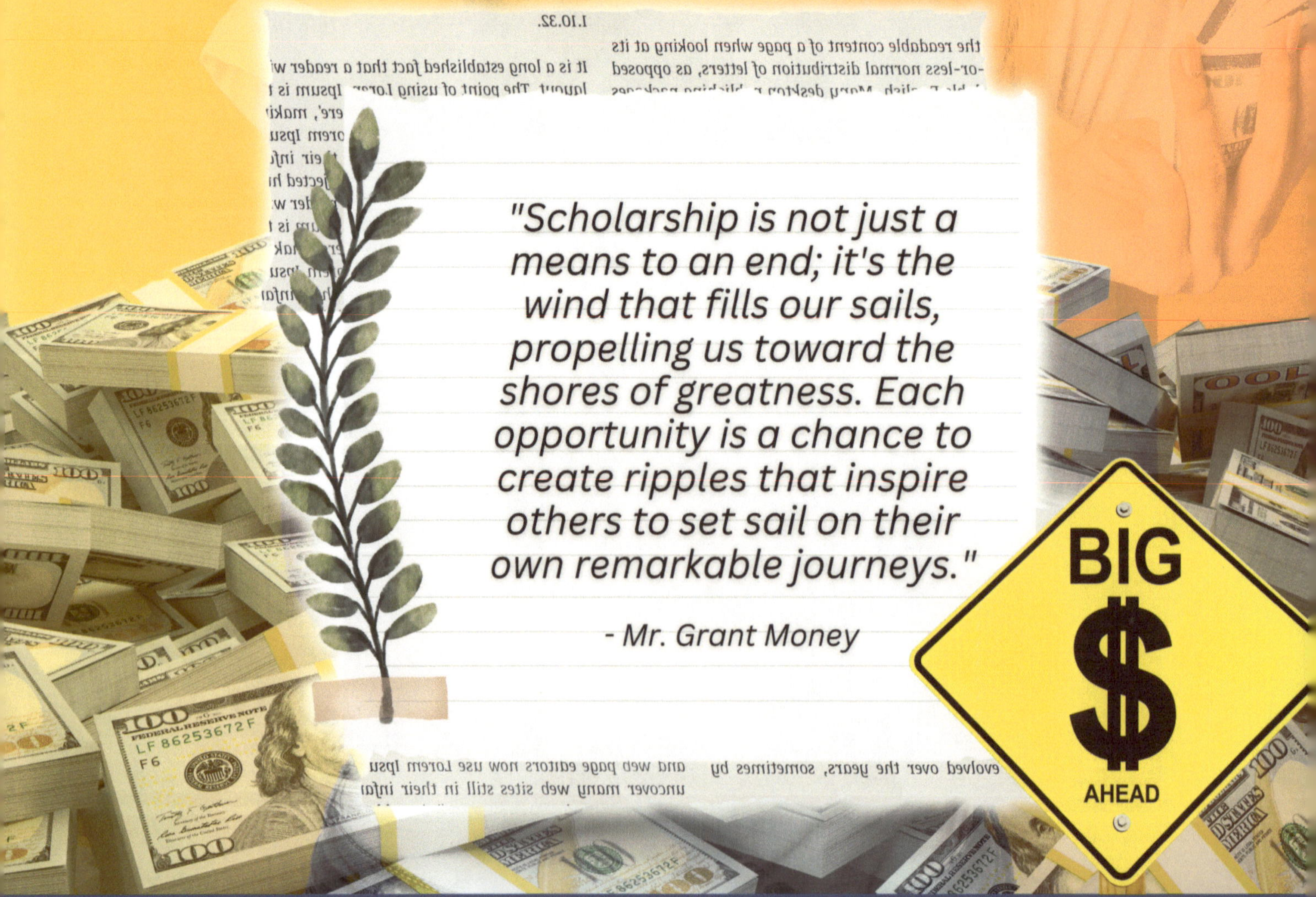

"Scholarship is not just a means to an end; it's the wind that fills our sails, propelling us toward the shores of greatness. Each opportunity is a chance to create ripples that inspire others to set sail on their own remarkable journeys."

- Mr. Grant Money

BIG $ AHEAD

Discussion Questions

1. How does Mr. Grant Money's catchphrase, "Today is a great day to make a great day," reflect his philosophy and positive outlook on life? How can adopting such a mantra impact one's mindset and actions?

2. Mr. Grant Money uses the acronym S.H.I.P to redefine the concept of scholarship as "Sailing High In Purpose." What other words or concepts could be redefined using acronyms to convey a deeper meaning? How might this linguistic technique influence our perception of those concepts?

3. Mr. Grant Money encourages the audience to view scholarships as opportunities to "sail high in purpose" and leave a positive wake of inspiration. In what ways can individuals leverage their achievements or opportunities to create positive ripples in their communities or fields of study? Share examples from your own experiences or observations.

4. Reflecting on Mr. Grant Money's childhood story about skipping rocks on the water and creating ripples, how can seemingly small actions or decisions in our lives lead to significant positive impacts? Can you recall a personal experience where a small choice had a ripple effect on your life or the lives of others?

5. Mr. Grant Money shares a poignant quote, "Scholarship is the wind in our sails, propelling us to create ripples that touch the shores of greatness." What are the symbolic meanings behind the elements of wind, sails, and shores in this metaphor? How might these elements relate to the pursuit of personal and academic success, and how can individuals harness these forces in their own journeys?

 Big Idea "S.H.I.P. Innovation Challenge"

Building upon Mr. Grant Money's acronym for scholarship, "Sailing High In Purpose," schools can organize the "S.H.I.P. Innovation Challenge." Students across various disciplines collaborate to develop innovative projects or solutions that contribute to the betterment of their communities or address global challenges. Whether it's creating sustainable technologies, implementing educational initiatives, or devising community outreach programs, the challenge encourages students to apply their skills and knowledge with a higher purpose in mind. This practical, hands-on approach not only reinforces the concept of scholarship as a force for positive change but also empowers students to actively contribute to society, echoing the theme of leaving a wake of inspiration.

🔍 Word Search

Welcome to the exciting "Mr. Grant Money Wordsearch Puzzle!" In this challenging word search, we've hidden 15 words related to a fascinating story about Mr. Grant and his adventures. As you embark on this word hunt, immerse yourself in the narrative and uncover the hidden gems that tell the tale of Mr. Grant's journey.

Can you find all the words and piece together the story that revolves around grant money? Let the puzzle-solving begin!

Now, here are the 15 words for the word search puzzle based on the story:

O	A	C	U	T	E	R	A	M	I	I	E	Y	O
S	C	H	M	C	T	I	V	T	A	N	V	I	P
U	T	A	E	V	E	I	H	C	A	I	O	T	P
C	R	L	V	O	O	E	U	G	C	I	R	L	O
C	I	L	Y	E	N	O	M	T	U	V	E	E	R
E	U	E	R	V	N	S	O	D	Q	N	P	R	T
S	M	N	A	R	V	R	R	P	S	T	S	U	U
S	P	G	M	P	Y	A	U	N	E	O	O	T	N
R	H	E	B	V	R	R	N	S	E	T	R	N	I
Q	E	I	I	N	S	G	O	N	L	M	P	E	T
U	E	I	T	U	G	O	A	L	F	A	A	V	Y
E	S	T	I	G	N	I	D	N	U	F	M	D	T
S	S	S	T	O	N	I	T	U	T	P	V	U	A	Q
T	V	I	N	M	T	N	A	R	G	R	G	R	T

Word list:

PURSUIT
QUEST
TRIUMPH
ACHIEVE
VICTORY
GRANT
CHALLENGE
ADVENTURE
SUCCESS
FUNDING
OPPORTUNITY
GOAL
AMBITION
PROSPER
MONEY

BRAZIL

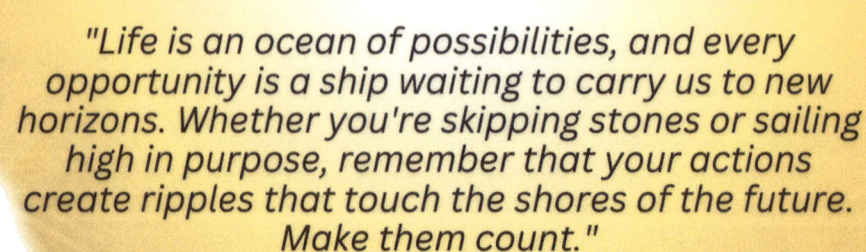

"Life is an ocean of possibilities, and every opportunity is a ship waiting to carry us to new horizons. Whether you're skipping stones or sailing high in purpose, remember that your actions create ripples that touch the shores of the future. Make them count."

SUCCESS STORIES

"Scholarship is the wind in our sails, propelling us to create ripples that touch the shores of greatness."

Princess, a young and ambitious traveler, had spent two weeks exploring the vibrant city of Rio de Janeiro. She was drawn to the enigmatic Mr. Grant Money, who exuded positivity and charisma wherever he went. His catchphrase, "Today is a great day to make a great day," resonated deeply with her, setting the stage for her own transformative journey.

Onboard the cruise ship, Princess recognized Mr. Grant Money and felt an immediate connection to his message of scholarship success. Inspired by his presence, she approached him with a burning question: "How can I embark on my own scholarship journey and create ripples of positive change?"

Mr. Grant Money, ever gracious and eager to inspire, shared his wisdom with Princess. He emphasized that scholarships were not just financial opportunities but pathways to personal growth and a chance to make a difference in the world. He encouraged her to think of scholarships as opportunities to "sail high in purpose" and create a wake of inspiration for others.

Princess listened intently, her heart and mind touched by Mr. Grant Money's words. She realized that her passion for travel and cultural exploration could be her ticket to scholarship success. She decided to pursue scholarships that aligned with her interests in international relations, languages, and cultural studies.

As the cruise ship sailed toward new horizons, Princess embarked on her scholarship journey with renewed determination. She delved into research, crafted compelling essays, and actively engaged with professionals in her desired field. Her commitment to creating ripples of positive change through her scholarship applications became her driving force.

Months later, Princess received the news she had been waiting for – she had been awarded a prestigious scholarship to study international relations and cultural studies. Her dreams of sailing high in purpose were becoming a reality.

Princess's success story became an inspiration to others onboard the cruise ship. She shared her journey and encouraged fellow travelers to pursue their passions and seek scholarship opportunities that resonated with their unique interests and aspirations. The cruise became a voyage of personal growth and scholarship discovery for many, all inspired by Princess's determination to create ripples of positive change.

As the cruise ship continued its journey, Princess gazed out at the endless horizon, her heart filled with gratitude for the opportunities that scholarships had brought into her life. She knew that she was not just sailing toward her dreams but also leaving behind a wake of inspiration for others to follow.

Chronicles of Scholarship: Unveiling History's Hidden Pages

Join Mr. Grant Money On An Epic Journey Through Time, Discovering The Untold Stories That Shaped Scholarships And Education

As Mr. Grant Money soared through the skies, leaving the vibrant colors of the Amazon River behind, he couldn't help but reflect on the incredible experiences of his journey. Dressed in a stylish black suit accented with a vibrant turquoise tie and a golden lapel pin shaped like an open book, he felt ready for the adventures that lay ahead.

The hum of the plane's engines created a soothing backdrop, and soon, Mr. Grant Money succumbed to the gentle rhythm, closing his eyes for a moment of rest. As he drifted into slumber, a vivid dream enveloped him.

In the dream, a colossal history book descended from the heavens, crashing to the earth with a resounding thud. Dust swirled around the impact, and as the particles settled, Jerla, his angelic guide, materialized in the form of a majestic eagle. With a regal flap of her wings, she soared into the pages of the book, and as she did, a cascade of money burst into the air like a dazzling display of fireworks.

Mr. Grant Money, captivated by the spectacle, felt a deep sense of purpose. He understood that Jerla was urging him to delve into the history of scholarships, to unearth the stories that shaped education and philanthropy in America.

Upon landing in Vancouver for the special conference, Mr. Grant Money wasted no time. The luxury hotel awaited, and with the energy of his dream propelling him forward, he delved into the history of scholarships.

As if guided by an unseen force, Mr. Grant Money found himself transported back in time. Each page he turned in the historical records revealed key moments that shaped the landscape of education and philanthropy in America. With his Golden Journal in hand, he meticulously chronicled these pivotal events:

1. Morrill Land-Grant Acts (1862 and 1890): Mr. Grant Money witnessed the signing of the Morrill Acts, which granted land to states for the establishment of colleges focused on agriculture and mechanical arts.

2. Formation of the Rockefeller Foundation (1913): He saw the birth of the Rockefeller Foundation, a philanthropic organization that played a crucial role in funding scholarships and supporting educational initiatives.

3. G.I. Bill (1944): The dream unveiled the signing of the G.I. Bill, a landmark legislation providing education benefits to World War II veterans, significantly expanding access to higher education.

4. Civil Rights Act (1964): Mr. Grant Money observed the passage of the Civil Rights Act, which played a pivotal role in opening educational opportunities to all, irrespective of race or gender.

5. Creation of Pell Grants (1972): He witnessed the establishment of Pell Grants, a federal program providing financial aid to low-income students, making higher education more accessible.

6. Internet Age and Online Scholarships (Late 20th Century): The dream fast-forwarded to the late 20th century, highlighting the advent of the internet, which revolutionized scholarship searches and applications.

7. Philanthropic Contributions in the 21st Century: Mr. Grant Money glimpsed the ongoing philanthropic efforts of individuals and organizations, each contributing to the scholarship landscape in unique ways.

With a sense of awe, Mr. Grant Money returned to the present, armed with a wealth of knowledge. His Golden Journal now bore witness to the history that shaped the scholarships he so passionately advocated for. The dream and the guidance of Jerla had revealed a rich tapestry of events that fueled his commitment to making a difference in the world.

As he prepared to take the stage at the Vancouver conference, Mr. Grant Money felt a renewed sense of purpose. He was not just a passenger on this journey but a steward of knowledge and a catalyst for positive change. The pages of history had unfolded before him, and now, he was ready to share the stories that could inspire others to sail high in purpose, creating ripples of impact in the world of scholarships.

As Mr. Grant Money stood before the eager audience at the Vancouver conference, a sea of faces awaiting his wisdom, he took a moment to soak in the atmosphere. The dream, the history, and the profound insights gained from both had fueled his passion for scholarships.

With a gleam in his eye and a confident smile, he opened his Golden Journal, the repository of knowledge acquired through time and dreams. The room hushed as he began to speak, his voice carrying the weight of the centuries.

"To understand scholarship," Mr. Grant Money declared, "you must navigate the currents of its rich history. Each page tells a story, and within those stories lies the key to unlocking a future where education knows no bounds. Scholarship is not merely a gift; it is a journey through time, a tapestry woven with the threads of opportunity, philanthropy, and the unwavering pursuit of knowledge."

The audience listened intently, the power of his words resonating in the room. Mr. Grant Money continued, "Just as a ship charts its course guided by the stars, scholarship charts a course guided by the luminaries of our shared history. So, set sail with purpose, and remember: to understand scholarship is to embrace the echoes of its past, navigating towards a brighter future for all."

With those words, Mr. Grant Money concluded his address, leaving the audience inspired and enlightened. The powerful quote hung in the air, a beacon guiding the way for those who sought to understand and perpetuate the transformative force of scholarships: "To understand scholarship, set sail on the currents of its rich history and chart a course toward a future where education knows no bounds."

Exercise: "Chart Your Scholarship Voyage"

Objective: This creative exercise aims to engage participants in reflecting on the themes of scholarship history, personal journeys, and the transformative power of education.

Materials Needed:
- Large sheets of paper or poster boards
- Markers, pens, and colored pencils
- Glue, scissors, and magazines or printed images
- Stickers, glitter, or any other decorative items (optional)

Instructions:

1. Introduction (5 minutes):
- Begin by summarizing the story of Mr. Grant Money's journey, emphasizing the key themes of scholarship history, the dream sequence, and the powerful quote about understanding scholarship through its rich history.

2. Discussion (10 minutes):
- Facilitate a brief discussion about the importance of understanding the history of scholarships and how it can inspire individuals to pursue education and make a positive impact.

3. Visualization (15 minutes):
- Encourage participants to close their eyes momentarily and visualize their scholarship voyage. What does it look like? Where does it take them? What significant moments or historical events shape their journey?

4. Creative Expression (30 minutes):
- Provide participants with large sheets of paper or poster boards.
- Instruct them to create a visual representation of their scholarship voyage. They can use markers, pens, colored pencils, and any other materials to illustrate key moments, symbols, and landmarks on their journey.
- Encourage participants to include elements inspired by the story, such as a golden journal, an eagle guide, or a representation of a significant historical event in scholarship.

5. Collage Time Capsule (20 minutes):

- Invite participants to cut out images from magazines or printouts that represent their dreams, aspirations, and the transformative power of education.
- Encourage them to create a collage time capsule on their poster boards, symbolizing their scholarship journey's past, present, and future.

6. Share and Reflect (10 minutes):

- Invite participants to share their creations with the group once everyone has completed their scholarship voyages.
- Facilitate a reflection session where individuals can discuss the symbolism in their artwork, the historical elements they incorporated, and what the exercise taught them about their personal journey.

7. Group Gallery Walk (15 minutes):

- Arrange the completed scholarship voyages for a group gallery walk around the room.
- Participants can stroll around, observing and appreciating their peers' unique interpretations and creativity.

This exercise allows participants to express their thoughts and feelings creatively and provides a tangible visual representation of the powerful themes from the story. It encourages self-reflection, sparks meaningful discussions, and fosters a sense of connection among participants.

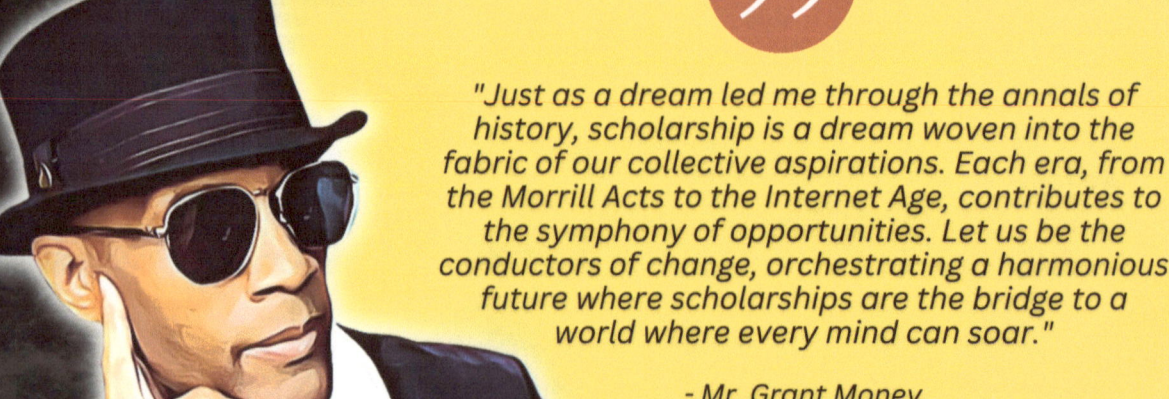

"Just as a dream led me through the annals of history, scholarship is a dream woven into the fabric of our collective aspirations. Each era, from the Morrill Acts to the Internet Age, contributes to the symphony of opportunities. Let us be the conductors of change, orchestrating a harmonious future where scholarships are the bridge to a world where every mind can soar."

- Mr. Grant Money

Discussion Questions

1. How did the historical events mentioned in Mr. Grant Money's dream, such as the Morrill Land-Grant Acts and the G.I. Bill, significantly shape the landscape of scholarships and access to education in the United States?

2. In the story, the Rockefeller Foundation and ongoing philanthropic efforts were highlighted. How has philanthropy played a role in the evolution of scholarships, and what impact do you think it continues to have on education today?

3. The Civil Rights Act of 1964 was a turning point in opening educational opportunities to all, regardless of race or gender. How have such legislative measures influenced the inclusivity of scholarships, and what challenges still exist in ensuring equal access to education?

4. The narrative fast-forwards to the late 20th century, marking the advent of the internet and online scholarships. In what ways have technological advancements, especially the internet, transformed the scholarship application process and accessibility to educational opportunities?

5. Mr. Grant Money emphasized the importance of individuals and organizations contributing to the scholarship landscape. How do individual efforts and collective contributions continue to shape scholarships in the 21st century, and what role can each person play in fostering positive change in education?

 Big Idea "Scholarship Futures Lab"

In the spirit of Mr. Grant Money's emphasis on navigating towards a brighter future, teachers and students can establish a "Scholarship Futures Lab." This dynamic and forward-thinking initiative involves brainstorming and developing creative ideas to address current challenges in education and scholarship accessibility. Students can form teams to explore emerging technologies, innovative funding models, or community-driven initiatives. The lab serves as a space for collaboration, experimentation, and problem-solving. By encouraging students to put their unique twist on scholarship concepts, the Scholarship Futures Lab empowers them to become catalysts for positive change in the landscape of education and philanthropy. This practical and hands-on approach not only instills a sense of agency but also prepares students for actively contributing to shaping the future of scholarships.

🔍 Word Search

Embark on a thrilling word search puzzle adventure inspired by the captivating journey of Mr. Grant Money, a charismatic explorer of scholarships and philanthropy. As he soared through the skies, delving into the history that shaped educational landscapes, Mr. Grant Money uncovered tales of generosity, innovation, and the unwavering pursuit of knowledge.

Join us in this puzzle as we celebrate the rich tapestry of scholarship history and the transformative impact it has had on education. Can you find the 15 hidden words that encapsulate the essence of Mr. Grant Money's dream-filled odyssey?

Now, here are the 14 words for the word search puzzle based on the story:

```
S I N T E R N E T L N P E E
O S O F E D E R A L O N E A
R S I L C I V I L I I C A R
T C T I E E A L E L T A N R
E H A I A C G I N L A E I O
L O D L R E E O B S L I R C
I L N S K H I S L I S O A K
N A U I L I S N K L I L M E
A R O S T O G T A G G T O F
I S F B I L L R C R E T R E
D H A I O L L L I A L S R L
O I C R I G H T S N N P I L
L P I N L P E L L T G D L E
A S L S O A L F A S I I L R
```

Word list:
ACTS
LEGISLATION
RIGHTS
BILL
ROCKEFELLER
GRANTS
INTERNET
ONLINE
SCHOLARSHIPS
FOUNDATION
CIVIL
PELL
AGE
MORRILL
FEDERAL

"Education, like a river, flows through the canyons of time, shaped by the historical forces that carve its path. Scholarships, akin to tributaries, feed into this river, nourishing the landscapes of minds and dreams. By understanding the currents of its rich history.

SUCCESS STORIES

"Summits of Scholarship: Mikkee's Journey to Educational Peaks with Mr. Grant Money"

Success is like climbing a mountain, and Mikkee was determined to conquer the highest peaks. Dressed in a rugged explorer's attire, he embarked on a life-changing journey to the Rocky Mountains of Colorado, where both nature's majesty and scholarship opportunities awaited him.

The mountains stood tall and imposing, a reflection of the challenges that lay ahead. But Mikkee, with unwavering resolve, took the first step. His quest was not merely to conquer the peaks but to reach new heights in education through scholarships.

As he ventured deeper into the wilderness, Mikkee discovered a hidden gem—an educational summit where scholars gathered to share knowledge and insights. Here, he met Mr. Grant Money, a seasoned scholar and mentor who had dedicated his life to helping others achieve their dreams.

Mr. Grant Money, dressed in a symbolic mountaineer's attire, became Mikkee's guide on this treacherous yet rewarding journey. He shared the wisdom of scholarship application strategies, teaching Mikkee to scale the peaks of essay writing, recommendation letters, and financial aid applications.

With each piece of advice, Mikkee felt more equipped to conquer the scholarship mountain. He learned to craft compelling narratives that highlighted his unique experiences and aspirations. He honed his networking skills, connecting with fellow scholars who shared his passion for education.

As the ascent continued, Mikkee encountered scholarship opportunities tailored to his interests in environmental conservation and sustainable agriculture. He applied diligently, leveraging his newfound knowledge and Mr. Grant Money's guidance to maximize his chances of success.

Finally, the day of reckoning arrived. Mikkee received the news he had been working tirelessly for—he had been awarded a prestigious scholarship that would not only fund his education but also provide the resources to make a meaningful impact in his chosen field.

Standing atop a metaphorical peak, Mikkee realized that success was indeed like climbing a mountain. It required determination, guidance, and the right tools. With Mr. Grant Money as his mentor and the Rocky Mountains as his backdrop, Mikkee had reached new educational heights, proving that with dedication and the right support, even the loftiest dreams could become a reality.

As Mikkee descended from the metaphorical summit, he knew that his journey was far from over. He had not only secured a scholarship but had also gained the knowledge and skills to continue scaling the mountains of success in his academic and professional life. The metaphorical mountain had been conquered, and Mikkee was ready to embrace the opportunities that lay ahead, driven by the belief that with perseverance and mentorship, he could reach even greater heights.

The Enchanted Journal: Mr. Grant Money's Scholarship Odyssey

Unveiling The Rich Tapestry Of Learning, Kindness, And Unexpected Adventures In Copenhagen

In the heart of Copenhagen, Denmark, where cobblestone streets whispered tales of centuries past, Mr. Grant Money strolled with purpose. Dressed in his classic stylish attire, a black suit complemented by a deep burgundy tie, he carried his Shirley Scepter—a symbol of his commitment to education and philanthropy. The air was alive with the city's rich history, and Mr. Grant Money immersed himself in its charm, visiting iconic attractions like the Little Mermaid statue, the colorful Nyhavn harbor, and the regal Amalienborg Palace.

As he explored the city's cultural tapestry, Mr. Grant Money felt a profound connection to its legacy of education and scholarship. Copenhagen's commitment to learning echoed through its architecture, its museums, and the very spirit of its people.

Seeking a quiet spot to reflect, Mr. Grant Money found respite in the lush surroundings of the King's Garden. Seated on a bench, he took a moment to delve into the depths of his own scholarship journey. Instead of beginning with the financial aid he received for college, he rewound the tape of time to his earliest experiences of support and inspiration.

In the recesses of his memory, he unearthed the moments when family, friends, and educators became the unsung heroes of his academic voyage. One memory shone brightly—an episode from his childhood involving Mrs. Golightly, his fifth and sixth-grade teacher. A beacon of kindness, she reached into her own pocket to fund an unforgettable Saturday on a ranch with horses and ranchers for her students.

The warmth of that experience, the genuine care, and the generosity left an indelible mark on Mr. Grant Money. With a smile, he acknowledged, "This too is a scholarship—a gift of experience and love that shaped me and continues to shape me. It is one of the reasons why I'm now paying it forward to inspire others."

In this quiet moment, amidst the greenery of the King's Garden, the realization dawned on him—the importance of exploring the history of scholarship over time and considering the myriad forms it could take. It wasn't merely about monetary aid for higher education; it was about the richness of experiences, the mentorship, and the moments that propelled individuals toward greatness.

An epiphany unfolded before Mr. Grant Money—an understanding that **education and scholarship reached far beyond the confines of a classroom.** It was a tapestry woven with threads of compassion, inspiration, and shared humanity.

He opened his Golden Journal, the pages awaiting the imprint of his insights. With careful consideration, he penned a powerful quote that encapsulated his newfound understanding: "Scholarship includes the sum of experiences, kindness, inspiration, and financial aid—a rich tapestry that not only shapes us but also influences others in ways we may not immediately recognize."

As he closed the journal, Mr. Grant Money felt renewed purpose. His future adventures, he mused, might reveal even more stories of those who had paid it forward, leaving an indelible mark on the world. With this realization, he stood up, once again ready to explore the enchanting streets of Copenhagen, inspired by the rich tapestry of scholarship that extended far beyond the traditional bounds of financial aid.

"In the corridors of time, the echoes of scholarship resound not just in the halls of academia but in the simple acts of kindness, the profound experiences, and the shared moments that weave the rich tapestry of education."
- Mr. Grant Money

Exercise: "The Scholarship Tapestry Collage"

Objective: This hands-on exercise aims to engage participants in reflecting on the diverse elements that make up the scholarship journey, including experiences, kindness, inspiration, and financial aid.

Materials Needed:
- Large sheets of paper or poster boards for each participant
- Magazines, newspapers, or printed images
- Scissors, glue, and colored markers
- Stickers, glitter, or any other decorative items (optional)

Instructions:

1. Introduction (5 minutes):
- Begin by summarizing the story of Mr. Grant Money's reflections in Copenhagen, emphasizing the idea that scholarship encompasses experiences, kindness, inspiration, and financial aid.

2. Discussion (10 minutes):
- Facilitate a brief discussion about the various elements of scholarship mentioned in the story and how they contribute to an individual's personal and academic growth.

3. Personal Reflection (10 minutes):
- Ask participants to take a few moments to reflect on their own scholarship journey. Encourage them to think about experiences, acts of kindness, moments of inspiration, and any financial aid that played a role in their educational path.

4. Collage Creation (30 minutes):
- Provide each participant with a large sheet of paper or poster board.
- Instruct them to create a "Scholarship Tapestry Collage" that visually represents the diverse elements of their scholarship journey. They can use images from magazines, newspapers, or printed materials to represent experiences, acts of kindness, moments of inspiration, and financial aid.
- Encourage participants to get creative with their collages, using colors, shapes, and decorations to convey the richness of their scholarship tapestry.

5. Share and Reflect (15 minutes):

- Invite participants to share their creations with the group after the collages are completed. Each person can briefly explain the significance of the elements they included in their collage.
- Facilitate a reflection session where participants discuss commonalities and unique aspects of their scholarship journeys.

6. Group Display and Appreciation (10 minutes):

- Arrange the completed collages around the room for a group display.
- Encourage participants to walk around, observe, and appreciate the diversity of scholarship journeys represented in the collages.

This interactive exercise allows participants to explore and celebrate the multifaceted nature of scholarship. It fosters self-reflection, encourages creative expression, and visualizes the collective tapestry of experiences, kindness, inspiration, and financial aid that shapes individuals' educational paths.

"As I walk through the pages of history in the cobblestone streets of Copenhagen, I realize that the true scholarship is a multifaceted gem it gleams not only in the gold of financial assistance but also in the vibrant hues of experiences, the nurturing touch of mentors, and the shared warmth of humanity. Education is a masterpiece painted with strokes of inspiration, kindness, and the relentless pursuit of knowledge."

- Mr. Grant Money

Discussion Questions

1. How does Mr. Grant Money's experience in the King's Garden in Copenhagen challenge conventional notions of scholarship, emphasizing the importance of experiences, mentorship, and shared humanity in addition to financial aid?

2. Reflecting on Mrs. Golightly's impact on Mr. Grant Money's childhood, how might educators and mentors play a crucial role in shaping an individual's scholarly journey, and how can their influence extend beyond the classroom?

3. In the context of Mr. Grant Money's quote, "Scholarship includes the sum of experiences, kindness, inspiration, and financial aid," how do you perceive the role of kindness and inspiration in shaping educational experiences, and how might they contribute to a broader understanding of scholarship?

4. Mr. Grant Money's realization suggests that the history of scholarship is a rich tapestry woven with threads of compassion. How can communities and societies foster a culture that values and supports diverse forms of scholarship beyond traditional academic pursuits?

5. Considering the Little Mermaid statue, Nyhavn harbor, and Amalienborg Palace as iconic attractions in Copenhagen, how might the cultural and historical context of a city influence and contribute to the development of individuals committed to education and philanthropy, as exemplified by Mr. Grant Money?

💡 Big Idea "Generosity Day" Event:

Taking inspiration from Mrs. Golightly's act of funding a special day for her students, schools could organize an annual "Generosity Day" event. On this day, teachers and students alike contribute small acts of kindness, mentorship, or unique experiences to their peers and colleagues. These acts may range from organizing workshops, sharing personal stories of inspiration, to creating mentorship opportunities. The aim is to cultivate a culture of generosity within the school community, recognizing that scholarship extends beyond financial aid and encompasses the giving of time, knowledge, and support. "Generosity Day" not only builds stronger connections among students and teachers but also reinforces the idea that everyone has something valuable to contribute to the educational journey.

🔍 Word Search

Embark on a word search journey inspired by the enchanting tale of Mr. Grant Money's exploration through the historic streets of Copenhagen. As he strolled through cobblestone pathways and immersed himself in the rich legacy of education and philanthropy.

Join Mr. Grant Money on this intellectual quest as you search for words that mirror the profound realization that education extends beyond the classroom into the realms of compassion and mentorship.

Now, here are the 15 words for the word search puzzle based on the story:

S	N	P	H	I	L	A	N	T	H	R	O	P	Y
C	H	G	O	L	D	E	N	A	G	I	E	U	I
H	N	I	N	A	L	T	A	P	E	S	T	R	Y
O	O	P	E	Y	A	R	S	O	E	L	H	P	L
L	I	T	X	T	N	T	C	I	G	T	G	I	D
A	T	H	P	U	R	P	E	D	N	E	N	H	H
R	A	O	N	O	U	N	P	T	T	L	I	S	U
S	C	N	S	S	O	C	T	E	T	T	R	M
H	U	T	U	T	J	C	E	E	P	P	N	O	A
I	D	N	H	N	T	O	R	E	S	I	A	T	N
P	E	X	P	E	R	I	E	N	C	E	H	N	I
N	O	I	T	A	R	I	P	S	N	I	C	E	T
R	L	A	I	C	N	A	N	I	F	H	N	M	Y
I	A	N	C	O	P	E	N	H	A	G	E	N	U

Word list:

JOURNAL
EXPERIENCE
EDUCATION
SCEPTER
HUMANITY
GOLDEN
ENCHANTING
PHILANTHROPY
FINANCIAL
INSPIRATION
TAPESTRY
COPENHAGEN
SCHOLARSHIP
MENTORSHIP

"Life's grand auction offers unique prizes to those who dare to bid on diverse experiences. Just as Mr. Grant Money embraced the thrill of speed, seize the opportunities with a blend of passion, strategy, and your own distinct flair."

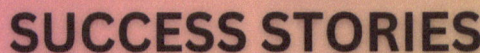

SUCCESS STORIES

"From Small Town to Global Stage: Julia's Scholarship Journey Towards Environmental Triumph"

The world was on the brink of disaster until Julia stepped onto the global stage. Dressed in a sharp, eco-friendly suit adorned with a green lapel pin symbolizing sustainability, she was a beacon of hope amidst environmental turmoil. The setting was a pivotal United Nations Climate Change Conference in Paris, where world leaders gathered to address the impending crisis.

Julia's journey to this defining moment had been anything but ordinary. Raised in a small town, her childhood was marked by an unyielding passion for the environment, cultivated during countless hikes in the nearby forest and summer days spent cleaning up local parks. However, her most formative experience occurred during her college years when she secured a scholarship dedicated to environmental advocacy.

This scholarship opened doors to prestigious institutions and mentorship opportunities, fueling Julia's commitment to environmental conservation. Armed with knowledge, she ventured into research, where her groundbreaking discoveries in renewable energy technologies captured the attention of both academia and industry leaders.

The turning point came when Julia was invited to address an international gathering of environmentalists. With unwavering determination and the support of her scholarship, she presented her innovative ideas to harness renewable energy sources, reducing carbon emissions and mitigating climate change.

Her impassioned speech garnered widespread acclaim, leading to invitations to various global forums. Her unique blend of scientific expertise and advocacy had transformed her into a trailblazing force for sustainability.

Back in Paris, as Julia addressed the United Nations delegates, her scholarship journey came full circle. Her visionary leadership and scientific acumen were instrumental in shaping a historic agreement to combat climate change. Her voice echoed through the conference halls, urging nations to adopt sustainable practices for the sake of future generations.

Julia's scholarship had not only paved her path to academic excellence but also empowered her to change the course of history. She stood as a testament to the transformative power of scholarships, demonstrating that with the right support, even the most daunting global challenges could be overcome.

As the conference concluded with a resounding commitment to environmental preservation, Julia left an indelible mark on the world. Her scholarship had propelled her from a small town to a global stage, where she had played a pivotal role in averting a climate disaster. Her story served as a beacon of inspiration for countless others, illustrating that with determination and scholarship support, anyone could become a catalyst for positive change on a global scale.

FROM SUBS TO SCHOLARS

The Amazing Adventures of
MRGRANTMONEY

From Subs to Scholars: Mr. Grant Money's Extraterrestrial Expedition

Join Mr. Grant Money In A Steamy Encounter With Aliens, Scholarships, And The Jazz Of Benevolence

In the tranquil paradise of St. Lucia, Mr. Grant Money found himself at a luxurious resort, surrounded by the beauty of sandy beaches and azure waters. Dressed in resort casual, he decided to take a quick sprint along the sun-kissed shoreline, absorbing the breathtaking scenery.

Feeling invigorated, Mr. Grant Money returned to the resort, deciding to indulge in some exercise and relaxation. He entered the steam room, the warm mist enveloping him as he settled onto the bench. As the steam worked its magic on his tired muscles, he began reflecting on his mission and the strategic plans to further its impact.

In the haze of the steam, Mr. Grant Money drifted into a steamy slumber, unsure if he had entered a dream or an otherworldly experience. Suddenly, he found himself surrounded by beings not of this world—aliens. Peculiarly, he felt a sense of calm, a knowing that this encounter held a deeper purpose.

The aliens communicated in a language unfamiliar to him, yet somehow, he understood. They transported him to a local sandwich shop, where a benevolent owner, Perry Joints, dedicated a day's profits to fund scholarships for students in the community. Mr. Grant Money, inside the store, adorned with posters of jazz legends like Miles Davis, felt the rhythm of Perry's generosity—a melody that resonated in his ears and heart.

The alien journey continued as they propelled Mr. Grant Money into the future, revealing the profound impact of Perry's scholarship initiative. The story of one student, Mia Williams, unfolded among the many lives.

Mia, a determined young woman who dreams of becoming a marine biologist, faced financial barriers to pursuing her education. The scholarship from Perry Joints' sandwich shop eased her financial burden and ignited a passion for environmental conservation. With the support of the scholarship, Mia went on to conduct groundbreaking research on marine biodiversity, leaving an indelible mark on the scientific community.

As Mr. Grant Money returned to the steam room, the aliens' presence faded. He looked around, questioning the reality of what he had just experienced. Was it a dream or a glimpse into a cosmic reality? Uncertain, he left the steam room, determined to record the extraordinary encounter in his Golden Journal.

A powerful quote echoed in his mind as he contemplated the impact of scholarships: "In the great tapestry of humanity, the threads of scholarships weave a story that transcends time and space—a story of empowerment, generosity, and the endless possibilities that unfold when we invest in the dreams of others."

Mr. Grant Money knew that the tales of Perry Joints and Mia Williams had to be shared. As he departed the resort, he carried a renewed determination to inspire students and business owners alike. His mission extended beyond monetary grants; it encompassed the profound ripple effects of meaningful contributions.

In the distance, the waves of St. Lucia's shore whispered, echoing the boundless potential that scholarships held in shaping a future where acts of kindness and generosity created a symphony of change.

Exercise: "Scholarly Sandwich Shop Challenge"

Objective: This engaging exercise encourages participants to think creatively about contributing to education and scholarships while drawing inspiration from the story of Perry Joints' sandwich shop.

Materials Needed:
- Large sheets of paper or poster boards
- Markers, pens, and colored pencils
- Magazines, newspapers, or printed images
- Scissors, glue, and decorative items
- Flip chart or whiteboard and markers

Instructions:

1. Introduction (10 minutes):
- Begin by summarizing the story of Mr. Grant Money's encounter with Perry Joints' sandwich shop and the impact it had on Mia Williams.
- Emphasize the theme of creative contributions to education and scholarships.

2. Brainstorming Session (15 minutes):
- Facilitate a group brainstorming session about creative ways local businesses can contribute to scholarships and education. Encourage participants to think outside the box.
- Write down ideas on a flip chart or whiteboard for everyone to see.

3. Personal Reflection (10 minutes):
- Ask participants to reflect on their own skills, resources, and networks. How could they contribute to scholarships uniquely and meaningfully, inspired by Perry Joints' sandwich shop?

4. Scholarly Sandwich Shop Design (30 minutes):
- Provide each participant with a large sheet of paper or poster board.
- Instruct them to create a "Scholarly Sandwich Shop" design that visually represents their creative contribution to scholarships. They can use images from magazines or draw illustrations to showcase their unique ideas.
- Encourage them to think about the theme, branding, and the specific way their business would contribute to educational initiatives.

5. Presentation and Discussion (20 minutes):
- Allow each participant to present their "Scholarly Sandwich Shop" design to the group. They can explain the concept, the impact they hope to achieve, and any creative elements they incorporate.
- Open the floor for discussion, allowing participants to share feedback, ask questions, and exchange ideas.

6. Gallery Walk (15 minutes):
- Arrange the completed "Scholarly Sandwich Shop" designs for a gallery walk around the room.
- Participants can walk around, observe, and appreciate the diverse and creative contributions imagined by their peers.

7. Reflection and Action Plan (10 minutes):
- Facilitate a reflection session where participants share their key takeaways from the activity.
- Encourage participants to create a simple action plan outlining how they can bring elements of their "Scholarly Sandwich Shop" design to life in their community.

This exercise sparks creativity and encourages participants to consider how they can make a meaningful impact on education and scholarships using their unique skills and resources. It fosters a sense of empowerment and showcases the diverse ways individuals can contribute to the scholarly tapestry.

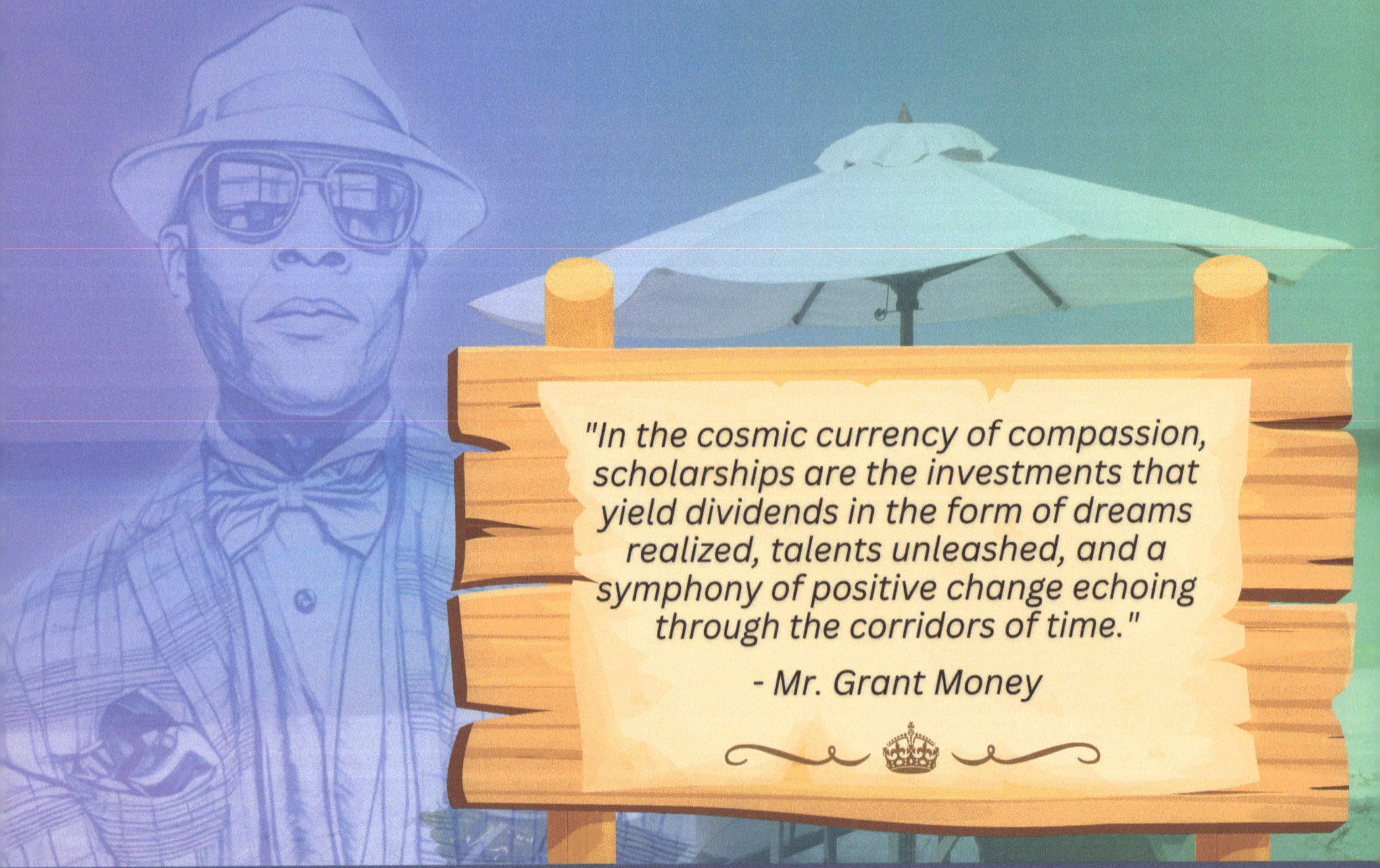

"In the cosmic currency of compassion, scholarships are the investments that yield dividends in the form of dreams realized, talents unleashed, and a symphony of positive change echoing through the corridors of time."

- Mr. Grant Money

Discussion Questions

1. Reflecting on Mr. Grant Money's experience, do you think encounters with extraterrestrial beings, even in dreams or otherworldly experiences, can have a profound impact on an individual's perspective and actions? How might such an encounter influence one's sense of purpose and mission in life?

2. The story emphasizes the transformative power of scholarships in Mia Williams' life. In your opinion, how do financial barriers impact individuals' pursuit of education and their ability to contribute to society? Can you think of other examples where financial support has played a pivotal role in shaping someone's future and the broader community?

3. Perry Joints, the sandwich shop owner, plays a crucial role in the story by dedicating a day's profits to fund scholarships. How can small businesses contribute to social causes in meaningful ways? What other creative approaches might businesses take to make a positive impact on their communities, and what role does the local community play in supporting such initiatives?

4. The aliens in the story communicate with Mr. Grant Money in an unfamiliar language, yet he understands their message. How does language, both verbal and non-verbal, influence communication and understanding among diverse individuals or beings? Can you share instances where you've experienced effective communication despite language barriers?

5. The narrative suggests that Mr. Grant Money's mission expanded beyond monetary grants to focus on the ripple effects of meaningful contributions. In your opinion, how can individuals and organizations create lasting impacts beyond financial aid? What are some examples of initiatives that go beyond monetary support and contribute to positive, long-term change in communities?

 Big Idea "Journey Journals" for Scholarships:

Students and teachers embark on a collaborative project to create "Journey Journals" that document their personal and academic growth. These journals become a collection of stories, dreams, and achievements, similar to Mr. Grant Money's Golden Journal. Students share their experiences, challenges, and aspirations, allowing the community to connect on a deeper level. The journals, creatively designed and filled with illustrations, are auctioned annually, with the proceeds funding scholarships for deserving students. This project not only promotes self-expression but also empowers students to contribute actively to the scholarship ecosystem.

🔍 Word Search

Welcome to the "Mr. Grant Money Wordsearch Puzzle," a captivating journey inspired by the extraordinary adventures of Mr. Grant Money in the tranquil paradise of St. Lucia. Immerse yourself in the story of a man whose mission goes beyond monetary grants, exploring the profound impact of scholarships on individuals and communities.

As you search for the hidden words, reflect on the power of generosity, dreams, and the boundless possibilities that unfold when we invest in the aspirations of others.

Now, here are the 15 words for the word search puzzle based on the story:

S	A	S	N	U	S	R	J	R	O	O	E	G	E
L	A	T	N	E	M	N	O	R	I	V	N	E	M
C	A	Z	U	R	E	S	I	I	E	R	A	N	S
O	E	G	I	J	P	T	O	T	G	V	S	E	P
G	X	S	I	O	N	L	N	T	M	B	O	R	I
R	E	E	L	I	A	N	R	L	H	E	T	O	H
A	R	N	U	N	Z	L	O	L	H	A	S	S	S
N	C	I	C	T	H	R	I	A	Y	C	I	I	R
T	I	R	I	S	T	P	O	E	G	H	G	T	A
M	S	A	A	I	R	U	I	H	N	E	O	Y	L
O	E	M	Y	A	O	R	G	M	A	S	L	N	O
N	E	G	R	I	S	O	E	E	I	N	O	S	H
E	I	E	R	E	E	O	R	R	N	C	I	B	C
Y	N	O	I	J	R	M	O	L	I	E	B	I	S

JOINTS
LUCIA
ENVIRONMENTAL
GENEROSITY
RESORT
ALIENS
GRANT
ROOM
SCHOLARSHIPS
MARINE
EXERCISE
BIOLOGIST
AZURE
MONEY
BEACHES

way to Beach →

"In the realm where dreams collide with generosity, a sandwich shop named Perry Joints became the compass guiding one young mind through the uncharted waters of education. Mia Williams, propelled by a scholarship, not only discovered the depths of marine biology but also unveiled the boundless capacity within every act of kindness to shape destinies."

SUCCESS STORIES

"From Small-Town Dreamer to Global Environmental Advocate: Theo's Journey of Scholarship Success and Sustainable Impact"

Have you ever wondered what it takes to achieve success? Theo certainly did. Growing up in a small town, he had big dreams of making a difference in the world, but the path to success seemed daunting. Dressed in his signature sharp suit and tie, Theo embarked on a journey of self-discovery, determined to overcome obstacles and turn his dreams into reality.

Theo's journey began when he secured a scholarship tailored to his passion for renewable energy and sustainability. This scholarship not only eased his financial burden but also provided mentorship opportunities that ignited his drive to pursue a career in environmental advocacy.

As he delved deeper into his studies, Theo uncovered groundbreaking solutions to address climate change. His innovative research earned him recognition within the academic community and caught the eye of prominent environmental organizations.

The turning point came when Theo was invited to speak at a global sustainability summit. With eloquence and passion, he presented his ideas on harnessing renewable energy sources to combat climate change. His speech resonated with the audience, and he was soon catapulted into the world of environmental leadership.

Back in his hometown, Theo became a local hero, inspiring the next generation with his scholarship success story. He started outreach programs to mentor aspiring young minds, emphasizing the importance of scholarships and dedication in achieving one's goals.

Theo's journey from a small-town dreamer to a global environmental advocate exemplified the transformative power of scholarships. His story served as a beacon of hope for countless others, illustrating that with perseverance and the right support, one could overcome obstacles and create a lasting impact on the world.

As Theo continued his mission to combat climate change and empower future leaders, he carried with him the profound belief that scholarships could unlock the potential of individuals, driving positive change and shaping a brighter future for all.

Symphony of Scholarships: Mr. Grant Money's Melodic Mission

In the heart of Vienna, Mr. Grant Money Orchestrates a Transformative Symphony, Uniting Education And The Arts In A Global Movement

In the enchanting city of Vienna, where the melodies of classical music filled the air, Mr. Grant Money found himself on a new adventure. Dressed in a tailored tuxedo, he explored the historic streets, visiting iconic landmarks like the Schönbrunn Palace and the grand Vienna State Opera.

Inspired by the city's rich cultural heritage, Mr. Grant Money decided to attend a classical concert at the famous Musikverein. As the orchestra filled the concert hall with harmonious tunes, he was struck by a revelation—the power of music to transcend barriers and unite people.

Energized by this realization, Mr. Grant Money embarked on a mission to blend the world of music and education. He collaborated with renowned musicians, educators, and philanthropists to create the "Symphony of Scholarships" initiative.

The initiative aimed to host benefit concerts where the proceeds would fund scholarships for talented young musicians and aspiring scholars. The idea was to not only support education but also to showcase the transformative impact of the arts.

The first concert was a resounding success, with the Vienna Philharmonic Orchestra lending their talents to the cause. As the audience applauded, Mr. Grant Money beamed with satisfaction, knowing that the beautiful music they had enjoyed would echo through the lives of the scholarship recipients.

However, the story took an unexpected turn when Mr. Grant Money received an invitation to an exclusive gathering in the heart of Vienna's historic district. Intrigued, he attended the event, only to find himself in the presence of a mysterious benefactor —an elderly woman named Elise von Sonata.

Elise, a lifelong patron of the arts, shared her vision of creating a scholarship fund specifically for students pursuing music and the performing arts. She believed that nurturing artistic talents could enrich individual lives and contribute to the city's cultural legacy.

Mr. Grant Money and Elise joined forces, combining their passion for education and the arts. Together, they organized a series of workshops, masterclasses, and performances, creating a vibrant community where aspiring musicians and scholars could thrive.

As the "Symphony of Scholarships" continued to resonate, the impact reached far beyond Vienna. The initiative expanded to other cities, showcasing the universal language of music in the service of education.

In the story's grand finale, Mr. Grant Money stood on a stage, surrounded by talented scholarship recipients who had flourished under the program. The melodies of success echoed as the students expressed their gratitude through the language they knew best —music.

With a heart full of joy, Mr. Grant Money knew that this symphony of scholarships was a harmonious addition to his mission. The story ended with him looking ahead to new horizons, where the transformative power of education and the arts would continue to create beautiful melodies in the lives of those who dared to dream.

"In the heart of Vienna, where the notes of opportunity danced in the air, I discovered that education and music compose a symphony of endless possibilities. The 'Symphony of Scholarships' is not just a melody; it's a crescendo of dreams transforming into reality."

- Mr. Grant Money

Exercise: "Harmony of Dreams: Scholarship Composition"

Objective: This creative exercise encourages participants to explore the intersection of music, education, and philanthropy by composing their own "Symphony of Dreams." Participants will symbolic represent their aspirations and contributions to scholarship through the language of music.

Materials Needed:
- Blank sheets of music paper or plain paper
- Pencils, markers, and colored pencils
- Access to a computer or music streaming service for background music (optional)

Instructions:

1. Introduction (10 minutes):
- Share the story of "Symphony of Scholarships: Mr. Grant Money's Melodic Mission" to set the tone for the activity.
- Emphasize the connection between music, education, and philanthropy as a powerful force for positive change.

2. Listening Session (15 minutes):
- Optionally, play a piece of classical or instrumental music that evokes a sense of inspiration. Encourage participants to close their eyes and immerse themselves in the music, allowing it to spark their creativity.

3. Reflection and Aspiration (10 minutes):
- Ask participants to reflect on their own aspirations and the impact they would like to make in the realm of education and scholarship.
- Prompt them to consider how the language of music can symbolize their dreams and contributions to the community.

4. Composing the Symphony (30 minutes):
- Distribute blank sheets of music paper or plain paper to each participant.
- Instruct participants to use symbols, drawings, or words to represent different aspects of their vision for a scholarship program that blends music and education.
- Each section of the composition can symbolize a unique element, such as collaboration, mentorship, scholarship recipients, or the overall impact on the community.

5. Sharing and Interpretation (20 minutes):
- Allow participants to share their "Symphony of Dreams" compositions with the group.
- As each person presents their work, encourage them to explain the symbolism behind each element and how it contributes to the overall harmony of their scholarship vision.

6. Reflection and Group Discussion (15 minutes):
- Facilitate a group discussion where participants reflect on the similarities and differences in their compositions.
- Discuss the power of using creative expressions, such as music, to convey complex ideas and aspirations in the realm of philanthropy and education.

7. Gallery Walk (10 minutes):
- Arrange the compositions around the room for a gallery walk.
- Participants can explore and appreciate their peers' unique interpretations and creativity.

This exercise stimulates creative thinking and provides a unique avenue for participants to express their dreams and aspirations in the context of scholarship and philanthropy. The symbolic language of music adds depth to their visions, creating a harmonious blend of creativity and purpose.

"Vienna taught me that the sweetest harmony is found when the chords of education and the strings of culture intertwine. The 'Symphony of Scholarships' isn't just about giving; it's about orchestrating a legacy that resonates in the hearts of those who dare to reach for the stars."

- Mr. Grant Money

Discussion Questions

1. Reflecting on the story's setting in Vienna, how do you think the city's rich cultural heritage and iconic landmarks influenced Mr. Grant Money's decision to create the "Symphony of Scholarships" initiative? How important is the connection between a location's cultural environment and the development of initiatives that blend arts and education?

2. The story highlights the transformative impact of music on individuals and the community. Do you believe that music, or the arts in general, has the power to transcend cultural and societal barriers? How might initiatives like the "Symphony of Scholarships" contribute to breaking down these barriers and fostering unity?

3. Elise von Sonata, the mysterious benefactor, plays a pivotal role in the story. How does her vision of creating a scholarship fund specifically for students in the performing arts align with or differ from Mr. Grant Money's broader initiative? What does this collaboration reveal about the importance of diverse perspectives in creating comprehensive educational programs?

4. The story takes an unexpected turn when Mr. Grant Money encounters Elise von Sonata. How do chance encounters and unexpected partnerships contribute to the success of social initiatives, especially in the realms of education and the arts? Can you think of real-world examples where unexpected collaborations have led to positive outcomes?

5. The "Symphony of Scholarships" expands beyond Vienna and becomes a universal initiative. In your opinion, what are the key factors that enabled the program's success in reaching other cities? How might cultural differences influence the reception and adaptation of such initiatives in diverse communities around the world?

 Big Idea "Symphony Showcase" Entrepreneurship Program

Taking inspiration from the collaboration between Mr. Grant Money and Elise von Sonata, an "Symphony Showcase" entrepreneurship program can be developed for students interested in both music and business. Students can learn the ins and outs of organizing benefit concerts, managing artists, and securing sponsorships to fund educational initiatives. This hands-on program would empower students to use their artistic passion as a catalyst for positive change, emphasizing the practical aspects of entrepreneurship while promoting the importance of giving back to the community. The program can culminate in a student-organized benefit concert where they apply their newfound skills and contribute to a charitable cause of their choice.

🔍 Word Search

Welcome to the "Mr. Grant Money Wordsearch Puzzle," an engaging exploration inspired by the incredible journey of Mr. Grant Money in the enchanting city of Vienna. Join us as we navigate the historic streets, iconic landmarks, and the transformative world of music and education.

This puzzle features 15 words related to Mr. Grant Money's mission to harmonize education and the arts through the "Symphony of Scholarships" initiative. Discover the hidden words that resonate with the melody of success and the universal language of music.

Now, here are the 15 words for the word search puzzle based on the story:

A	P	H	I	L	H	A	R	M	O	N	I	C	E
O	S	C	H	O	L	A	R	S	H	I	P	P	R
N	R	N	P	E	R	F	O	R	M	A	N	C	E
M	C	M	Y	T	I	N	U	M	M	O	C	M	R
U	L	H	A	T	I	S	M	E	O	S	S	E	O
S	T	R	A	S	R	A	H	L	A	O	E	D	D
I	P	E	R	V	T	E	A	O	O	N	H	U	E
K	O	O	A	I	N	E	M	D	M	A	I	C	X
V	H	N	I	E	N	I	R	Y	U	T	S	A	U
E	S	A	L	N	E	A	A	C	H	A	E	T	T
R	K	E	M	N	S	U	M	D	L	S	L	I	R
E	R	A	E	A	N	Y	S	N	I	A	L	O	A
I	O	O	O	A	I	E	R	L	C	E	S	N	V
N	W	E	A	R	T	S	E	H	C	R	O	S	N

MASTERCLASS
PERFORMANCE
VIENNA
PHILHARMONIC
ELISE
TUXEDO
ARTS
SCHOLARSHIP
MELODY
MUSIKVEREIN
ORCHESTRA
EDUCATION
COMMUNITY
SONATA
WORKSHOP

"In the timeless city of Vienna, where every cobblestone tells a story, a beautiful symphony of generosity and passion unfolded. The 'Symphony of Scholarships,' conducted by Mr. Grant Money and Elise von Sonata, became a testament to the transformative power of collaboration and the enduring melody of shared dreams."

"Rising Sun Dreams: The Tokyo Tech Scholars Odyssey of Zian - A Tale of Perseverance, Innovation, and Global Impact"

In the bustling city of Tokyo, amidst the neon lights and the hum of modernity, a defining moment awaited Zian. Dressed in a sleek business suit, he had arrived in Japan's capital with a dream in his heart and determination in his eyes. As he navigated the crowded streets and towering skyscrapers, Zian couldn't help but reflect on the journey that had brought him here.

Growing up in a modest neighborhood, Zian had faced his fair share of challenges. His family struggled to make ends meet, and the path to higher education seemed like an insurmountable mountain. But Zian had a relentless spirit and an unwavering belief in the power of education to change lives.

One fateful day, as Zian was browsing the internet for scholarship opportunities, he stumbled upon the "Tokyo Tech Scholars" program—an initiative by the prestigious Tokyo Institute of Technology aimed at supporting talented international students. The prospect of studying in Japan's renowned institution filled Zian with hope.

With unwavering determination, Zian poured his heart into the scholarship application. He meticulously crafted essays that showcased his passion for robotics and artificial intelligence, fields he aspired to master. He knew that this scholarship could be his ticket to a brighter future, not only for himself but for his family as well.

Months passed, and Zian's anticipation grew. The day of the scholarship results arrived, and he could hardly contain his excitement. As he opened the email notification, tears of joy streamed down his face—he had been awarded the Tokyo Tech Scholars scholarship. It was a life-changing moment that marked the beginning of a remarkable journey.

Zian's years at Tokyo Tech were filled with rigorous academics, research endeavors, and cultural immersion. He dedicated himself to his studies, excelling in his chosen field. But it wasn't just the academic excellence that defined his success. Zian embraced the Japanese culture, learned the language, and formed deep connections with fellow scholars from around the world.

Upon graduation, Zian returned to his home country as a highly skilled engineer and innovator. His experiences in Tokyo had not only equipped him with technical expertise but also with a global perspective and a commitment to giving back.

Zian founded a startup focused on developing cutting-edge technologies that would revolutionize the robotics industry. His innovations gained international recognition, and his company became a symbol of success, rooted in the values of hard work, education, and gratitude.

Zian's journey from a challenging upbringing to becoming a pioneering entrepreneur was a testament to the transformative power of scholarships and the unwavering spirit of an individual determined to make a difference. His story served as an inspiration to countless young minds, reminding them that with dedication and the right opportunities, they too could reach new heights and contribute to a brighter future for themselves and their communities.

The Amazing Adventures of
MRGRANTMONEY
THE GOLDEN HARVEST

The Golden Harvest: Nurturing Dreams, Cultivating Futures

Uncover The Incredible Story of Mr. Grant Money And The Scholarship Seeds Of Hope Movement

In the vibrant city of Atlanta, beneath the towering skyscrapers and amidst the rhythm of life, Mr. Grant Money found himself pondering an idea that had sprouted from the fertile grounds of his Golden Journal. The notion was simple yet profound—what if every entity, big or small, made it their mission to sow the seeds of scholarships annually, cultivating a garden of educational opportunities?

As Mr. Grant Money strolled through Centennial Olympic Park, he gazed upon the fountain, its water droplets creating ripples that danced in the sunlight. The symbolism struck him—each scholarship could be a droplet, creating a ripple effect of education and hope. Inspired by this revelation, he decided to develop a plan to bring this vision to fruition.

Mr. Grant Money recognized that the key to turning this vision into reality lay in the hearts and minds of the youth. With a glimmer of excitement in his eyes, he embarked on a mission to ignite the spark of philanthropy and scholarship advocacy among young minds.

Partnering with local schools and youth organizations, Mr. Grant Money organized a Youth Rally at the heart of Atlanta. The event buzzed with youthful energy as students from different backgrounds gathered, eager to be part of something larger than themselves.

Mr. Grant Money took the stage, clad in his characteristic sharp attire, and shared his dream of a world where scholarships flowed abundantly, nourishing the aspirations of countless students. He spoke of the raindrop ripple effect, and the room resonated with the potential impact.

Mr. Grant Money unveiled his plan—a blueprint for youth-led scholarship advocacy. The idea was simple: students would be the ambassadors, approaching local businesses, corporations, civic organizations, fraternities, churches, faith-based organizations, and nonprofits, encouraging them to establish annual scholarships.

To everyone's amazement, the youth embraced the plan with fervor. Armed with passion and purpose, they formed Scholarship Seeds of Hope teams, each dedicated to approaching different entities in the community. Mr. Grant Money provided them with tools—guidelines, success stories, and the essence of why scholarships mattered.

The movement gained momentum as businesses and organizations, moved by the sincerity and enthusiasm of the young advocates, began to join the cause. Annual scholarships sprouted like seeds, creating a network of educational opportunities that reached every corner of Atlanta.

In the following years, the ripple effect became evident. Students who once doubted their ability to pursue higher education found themselves recipients of unexpected scholarships. Families experienced the transformative power of education, and communities thrived as more students pursued their dreams.

In a moment of quiet reflection, Mr. Grant Money felt a gentle breeze, as if Jerla herself whispered, "The raindrop ripples have turned into waves of change." The youth had sparked a movement and created a culture of scholarship advocacy that transcended generations.

As Mr. Grant Money observed the flourishing garden of scholarships, he marveled at the collaborative effort that had birthed it. In his Golden Journal, he penned a quote that captured the essence of the Scholarship Seeds of Hope movement: "In the hands of the youth, every seed becomes a scholarship, and every scholarship, a beacon of hope for a brighter tomorrow."

Exercise: "Seeds of Scholarship Workshop"

Objective: This workshop encourages participants to brainstorm, plan, and initiate a youth-led scholarship advocacy campaign in their community inspired by the "Scholarship Seeds of Hope" story.

Materials Needed:
- Large sheets of paper or poster boards
- Markers, pens, and colored pencils
- Sticky notes
- Flip chart or whiteboard and markers
- A space for group discussions

Instructions:

1. Introduction (15 minutes):
- Share the "Scholarship Seeds of Hope" story to set the context for the workshop.
- Emphasize the power of youth-led initiatives in creating positive change.

2. Brainstorming Session (20 minutes):
- Facilitate a group brainstorming session on the potential impact of youth-led scholarship advocacy.
- Encourage participants to generate ideas for approaching local entities and creating a culture of scholarship support.

3. Idea Sorting (15 minutes):
- Have participants write each idea on a sticky note.
- Create a visual display on a whiteboard or flip chart where participants can place their sticky notes, sorting ideas into categories such as outreach, communication, and collaboration.

4. Developing the Plan (30 minutes):
- Divide participants into small groups.
- Instruct each group to choose one or more ideas from the display and develop a detailed plan. They should consider the target entities, communication strategies, and potential challenges.

5. Group Presentations (30 minutes):
- Each group presents their scholarship advocacy plan to the entire group.
- Emphasize the importance of creativity, feasibility, and community involvement in their proposals.

6. Feedback and Collaboration (20 minutes):
- After each presentation, encourage feedback and suggestions from the rest of the participants.
- Facilitate collaboration between groups to enhance and refine ideas.

7. Selection of Promising Plan (15 minutes):
- Collectively discuss the strengths and weaknesses of each plan.
- Facilitate a group decision to select the most promising scholarship advocacy plan based on impact, feasibility, and creativity.

8. Action Steps and Commitment (30 minutes):
- Instruct participants to outline specific action steps for implementing the chosen plan.
- Encourage a commitment from each participant to actively contribute to the execution of the plan.

9. Mock Outreach Session (20 minutes):
- Conduct a mock outreach session where participants practice approaching local entities and presenting the scholarship advocacy initiative.
- Provide constructive feedback and tips for effective communication.

10. Reflection and Journaling (15 minutes):
- Provide time for individual reflection and journaling. Participants can write down their thoughts on the workshop, what they learned, and their personal commitment to implementing youth-led scholarship advocacy.

11. Closing Thoughts (10 minutes):
- Conclude the workshop by summarizing key takeaways and expressing optimism for the impact participants can collectively create.
- Encourage participants to stay connected and share their progress in implementing the scholarship advocacy plan.

This "Seeds of Scholarship Workshop" empowers participants to translate inspiration into action, fostering a sense of responsibility and leadership in advocating for educational opportunities in their community.

Discussion Questions

1. What role do you think symbolism played in Mr. Grant Money's vision, particularly the analogy of scholarships as water droplets creating a ripple effect? How can powerful metaphors like this inspire individuals and communities to take action?

2. Mr. Grant Money's plan relied on engaging youth as ambassadors for scholarship advocacy. How important do you believe it is to involve young people in social and philanthropic movements, and what unique perspectives and strengths do they bring to such initiatives?

3. In the story, businesses and organizations joined the cause after being approached by the youth advocates. What factors do you think contributed to their willingness to participate, and how can similar partnerships be fostered in real-world scenarios to support educational initiatives?

4. Reflecting on the impact of the Scholarship Seeds of Hope movement, what lessons can be drawn about the transformative power of education on individuals, families, and communities? How might this story inspire similar initiatives in other cities or regions?

5. The story emphasizes the collaborative effort that led to the flourishing garden of scholarships. In your opinion, how can communities effectively come together to address educational challenges, and what obstacles might they need to overcome in the process?

 Big Idea "Scholarship Creation Challenge"

Transform Mr. Grant Money's vision into an interactive and educational challenge for students. Teachers can encourage students to form teams and participate in a "Scholarship Creation Challenge," where they develop comprehensive proposals for establishing annual scholarships. Students would need to research potential sponsors, create persuasive presentations, and outline the impact of their proposed scholarships. This not only enhances critical thinking and research skills but also instills a sense of entrepreneurship and philanthropy.

🔍 Word Search

Welcome to the "Mr. Grant Money Wordsearch Puzzle," where you can explore the inspiring story of philanthropy, education, and the transformative power of scholarships in the vibrant city of Atlanta.

Join Mr. Grant Money on his journey as he envisions a world where every entity contributes to the growth of educational opportunities through the Scholarship Seeds of Hope movement.

Now, here are the 15 words for the word search puzzle based on the story:

S	A	J	H	F	C	F	J	B	E	A	C	O	N
Y	P	O	R	H	T	N	A	L	I	H	P	C	S
U	P	U	B	N	O	E	E	E	I	I	S	H	S
A	S	R	E	B	A	R	D	R	E	C	P	S	R
H	U	N	T	U	T	U	U	E	M	E	I	K	O
O	E	A	N	A	N	I	C	W	N	N	H	Y	D
P	R	L	I	S	A	R	A	O	I	T	S	S	A
E	A	I	R	A	L	P	T	P	A	E	R	C	S
A	J	I	P	R	T	U	I	P	T	N	A	R	S
C	N	A	E	P	A	O	O	P	N	N	L	A	A
F	N	O	U	A	L	R	N	L	U	I	O	P	B
O	S	O	L	R	N	E	A	O	O	A	H	E	M
C	B	A	B	N	R	H	L	P	F	L	C	R	A
Y	A	Y	O	U	T	H	U	A	R	C	S	S	N

EDUCATIONAL
SCHOLARSHIPS
JOURNAL
POWER
CENTENNIAL
RIPPLE
HOPE
AMBASSADORS
BEACON
PHILANTHROPY
YOUTH
FOUNTAIN
BLUEPRINT
ATLANTA
SKYSCRAPERS

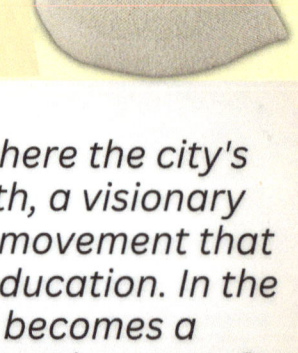

"Amidst the rhythms of Atlanta, where the city's heartbeat echoes through its youth, a visionary named Mr. Grant Money sparked a movement that forever changed the landscape of education. In the hands of the youth, every seed becomes a scholarship, and every scholarship, a beacon of hope for a brighter tomorrow. "

SUCCESS STORIES

"From Adversity to Advocacy: Moira's Inspirational Journey of Educational Triumph and Community Empowerment"

"I remember the day I decided to change my life," Moira began, her voice steady and determined. She stood before a captivated audience, sharing her remarkable journey to success. Dressed in a professional attire, she exuded confidence and grace as she recounted her path from adversity to triumph.

Growing up in a small, tight-knit community in rural Oklahoma, Moira faced her fair share of challenges. Limited access to quality education and economic hardships were constants in her life. But her indomitable spirit refused to yield to these obstacles.

Moira's turning point came during her senior year of high school when she stumbled upon a flyer for a scholarship workshop led by none other than Mr. Grant Money. Intrigued by the prospect of securing financial aid for college, she decided to attend the workshop, even though it meant a long journey to the nearest city.

Under Mr. Grant Money's guidance, Moira learned the intricacies of scholarship applications, essay writing, and interview skills. She soaked in every piece of advice like a sponge, determined to seize the opportunities that education could offer. The workshop was a pivotal moment—a spark that ignited her passion for higher learning.

With newfound knowledge and determination, Moira embarked on a scholarship application frenzy. She poured her heart into crafting essays that revealed her dreams, aspirations, and unwavering commitment to breaking the cycle of poverty in her family. The hard work paid off when she received her first scholarship offer—a lifeline to a brighter future.

Moira's journey didn't stop there. She secured additional scholarships and enrolled in a prestigious university. There, she majored in business administration, determined to leverage her education to create economic opportunities for herself and her community. Moira's grit and resilience made her a standout student, earning her mentorships and internships that further bolstered her skills.

Upon graduation, Moira was armed not only with a degree but also with a deep sense of purpose. She returned to her hometown, where she founded a nonprofit organization focused on providing scholarship resources and mentorship to underprivileged youth. Moira's story of triumph over adversity and her commitment to giving back inspired her community.

Moira concluded her speech with a heartfelt quote that encapsulated her journey: "I remember the day I decided to change my life. But I also remember the countless hands that reached out to help me along the way. Success is not a solitary journey; it's the result of collective support and unwavering determination."

As Moira received a standing ovation from the audience, she knew that her story had the power to inspire others to overcome their challenges, seize opportunities, and create a brighter future not only for themselves but for their communities as well.

The Green Thumb Scholarship: Growing Dreams, Harvesting Hope

Unearth The Transformative Journey Of Lily Greenfield's Educational Oasis In Bloomsville

In the vibrant town of Bloomsville, nestled between rolling hills and meadows, Mr. Grant Money found himself captivated by the stories of a high school student named Lily Greenfield. Dressed in a denim jacket adorned with patches of colorful flowers, Lily was not just an ordinary student—she was a visionary.

One sunny afternoon, Mr. Grant Money visited Bloomsville High School, where he discovered Lily passionately tending to a community garden. Inspired by her love for horticulture and a desire to make education accessible, Lily had embarked on a mission to create the "Green Thumb Scholarship."

Lily's vision was simple yet profound. She believed that the act of cultivating the earth could nurture both plants and human potential. She transformed a neglected plot of land near the school into a thriving community garden, with each plant symbolizing a student's dream waiting to blossom.

Lily's creativity knew no bounds. She organized gardening workshops, inviting community members to learn the art of cultivating greenery. Participants paid a small fee, and all proceeds went toward the Green Thumb Scholarship. Lily's dedication turned the garden into a buzzing hub of activity, with neighbors and students alike gathering to share knowledge and stories.

But Lily didn't stop there. Leveraging social media, she initiated a "Bloomsville Blooms" campaign, encouraging people to sponsor a plant in the garden. Sponsors received updates on their chosen plant's growth and, in return, contributed to the scholarship fund. The town rallied behind Lily's cause, making the garden a symbol of community unity and educational support.

As the garden flourished, so did the Green Thumb Scholarship. Lily's innovative approach cultivated a thriving community space and harvested an impressive $10,000 for scholarships. The funds were awarded to students demonstrating a passion for environmental sustainability and a commitment to community service.

One of the scholarship recipients, Carlos Mendez, had dreams of becoming an environmental scientist. The scholarship alleviated his financial burden and connected him with mentors in the field. With Lily's guidance, he planted the seeds of change in Bloomsville, initiating projects to improve local green spaces and promote eco-friendly practices.

Impressed by Lily's initiative, Mr. Grant Money visited Bloomsville High School to witness firsthand the Green Thumb Scholarship's impact. Lily welcomed him to the garden, where the air was filled with the fragrance of blooming flowers and the palpable sense of community achievement.

As Lily shared the success stories of scholarship recipients, Mr. Grant Money realized the profound impact that one student's creativity and determination could have on an entire community. The Green Thumb Scholarship had not only made education accessible but had also cultivated a sense of pride and collaboration among the people of Bloomsville.

Leaving Bloomsville, Mr. Grant Money carried with him the story of Lily Greenfield—a testament to the transformative power of individual initiative. The Green Thumb Scholarship was more than a financial aid program; it was a symbol of how creativity, community, and a passion for education could bloom together.

In his Golden Journal, Mr. Grant Money penned a quote inspired by Lily's story: "In the garden of dreams, the seeds of scholarship grow, nurtured by the hands of those who dare to cultivate a future of possibilities."

Exercise: "Budding Scholars Workshop"

Objective: This interactive workshop encourages participants to explore creative ways of fundraising for scholarships and fostering community involvement. Inspired by Lily Greenfield's initiative, participants will brainstorm and plan their own unique scholarship fundraising projects.

Materials Needed:
- Large sheets of paper or poster boards
- Markers, pens, and colored pencils
- Magazines, newspapers, or printed images
- Scissors, glue, and decorative items
- Flip chart or whiteboard and markers

Instructions:

1. Introduction (10 minutes):
- Share the story of Lily Greenfield and the Green Thumb Scholarship to introduce the theme of student-led scholarship initiatives.
- Emphasize the importance of creativity, community engagement, and the impact of small-scale initiatives.

2. Brainstorming Session (15 minutes):
- Facilitate a group brainstorming session on potential scholarship fundraising projects. Encourage participants to think creatively about their skills, interests, and community resources.
- Write down ideas on a flip chart or whiteboard for everyone to see.

3. Personal Reflection (10 minutes):
- Ask participants to reflect on their own skills and passions. How could they contribute to scholarship fundraising uniquely and meaningfully, considering the resources available to them?

4. Project Planning (30 minutes):
- Provide each participant with a large sheet of paper or poster board.
- Instruct them to plan and design their own scholarship fundraising project. They can use images from magazines, draw illustrations, or write down key details about their initiative.
- Encourage participants to consider the target audience, fundraising methods, and the overall theme of their project.

5. Sharing and Feedback (20 minutes):
- Allow each participant to present their scholarship fundraising project to the group. They can explain the concept, the impact they hope to achieve, and any creative elements they incorporated.
- Open the floor for feedback and suggestions from the group.

6. Gallery Walk (15 minutes):
- Arrange the project plans around the room for a gallery walk.
- Participants can stroll around, observe, and appreciate the diverse and creative fundraising ideas presented by their peers.

7. Reflection and Action Plan (10 minutes):
- Facilitate a reflection session where participants share their key takeaways from the activity.
- Encourage participants to create a simple action plan outlining how they can begin implementing their scholarship fundraising project in their community.

This interactive workshop stimulates creative thinking and empowers participants to actively contribute to scholarship initiatives. It fosters a sense of agency and demonstrates how individuals, inspired by stories like Lily Greenfield's, can make a meaningful impact on education and the community.

> *"Vienna taught me that the sweetest harmony is found when the chords of education and the strings of culture intertwine. The 'Symphony of Scholarships' isn't just about giving; it's about orchestrating a legacy that resonates in the hearts of those who dare to reach for the stars."*
>
> *- Mr. Grant Money*

Discussion Questions

1. How did Lily Greenfield's innovative approach to creating the Green Thumb Scholarship not only provide financial aid for students but also foster a strong sense of community engagement and collaboration in Bloomsville?

2. In what ways did the "Bloomsville Blooms" campaign leverage social media to connect the community with the Green Thumb Scholarship, and how did this initiative contribute to the success of the scholarship fund?

3. Explore the role of mentorship in the story, particularly in Carlos Mendez's journey as a scholarship recipient. How did mentorship contribute to his success in becoming an environmental scientist, and how did it further amplify the impact of the Green Thumb Scholarship?

4. Discuss the symbolism behind Lily Greenfield's community garden, where each plant represented a student's dream waiting to blossom. How did this creative vision contribute to the overall success of the Green Thumb Scholarship, and what broader message does it convey about the intersection of nature, education, and personal growth?

5. Mr. Grant Money's quote, "In the garden of dreams, the seeds of scholarship grow, nurtured by the hands of those who dare to cultivate a future of possibilities," suggests a profound connection between dreams and education. How does Lily Greenfield's story exemplify the transformative power of individual initiative in creating opportunities for others and shaping the future of a community?

 Big Idea "Scholarship Cultivation Workshops" for Students:

Inspired by Lily's gardening workshops, schools can organize scholarship cultivation workshops where students explore their passions and talents, transforming them into viable projects. These workshops could cover various areas like entrepreneurship, community service, or environmental sustainability. Students would not only develop practical skills but also learn how to turn their interests into initiatives that benefit both themselves and their communities. The funds generated from these projects could contribute to scholarships, creating a self-sustaining cycle of education and community support.

🔍 Word Search

Welcome to the "Mr. Grant Money Wordsearch Puzzle," where we celebrate the inspirational story of Lily Greenfield and the transformative power of the Green Thumb Scholarship in the vibrant town of Bloomsville. Lily, with her visionary spirit, turned a neglected plot into a thriving community garden, cultivating not just plants but the dreams of aspiring students.

Can you find them all in the word search puzzle? Immerse yourself in this tale of creativity, community, and the enduring impact of education.

Now, here are the 14 words for the word search puzzle based on the story:

N	O	E	L	I	L	Y	E	L	M	I	T	T	R
I	T	O	O	P	T	I	N	T	E	C	H	E	I
C	A	R	L	O	S	P	V	O	N	O	T	D	Z
R	V	T	I	S	L	I	I	T	T	M	A	U	R
F	T	I	N	S	V	H	R	E	O	M	G	C	Y
E	E	A	I	I	G	S	O	P	R	U	A	A	I
I	T	E	T	B	R	R	N	B	S	N	R	T	F
R	O	A	I	I	E	A	M	A	I	I	D	I	L
F	S	N	A	L	E	L	E	C	T	T	E	O	O
S	E	G	T	I	N	O	N	I	I	Y	N	N	S
E	O	H	I	T	G	H	T	M	E	N	D	E	Z
N	I	I	V	I	T	C	A	I	E	E	S	S	P
T	E	M	E	E	E	S	L	L	E	N	O	E	S
T	R	A	N	S	F	O	R	M	A	T	I	V	E

Word List:

- POSSIBILITIES
- MENDEZ
- SCHOLARSHIP
- TRANSFORMATIVE
- EDUCATION
- MENTORS
- ENVIRONMENTAL
- CARLOS
- GARDEN
- COMMUNITY
- INITIATIVE
- GREEN
- LILY

"Education is the garden where minds bloom, and in Bloomsville, Lily Greenfield has shown us that every student, like a carefully tended plant, has the potential to flourish and contribute to the vibrant landscape of our shared future."

SUCCESS STORIES

"From Small Town Dreamer to Empowering Entrepreneur: Belle's Journey of Passion, Perseverance, and Paying It Forward"

"Are you ready to transform your life?" Belle's words echoed through the room as she stood before an audience, exuding confidence and determination. Dressed in a sharp business suit, she radiated a sense of purpose that left everyone captivated.

Belle's journey to success began in a small town where opportunities were limited, but her aspirations knew no bounds. Armed with a dream and an unshakable belief in herself, she set out on a mission to create her path to success.

With little more than a laptop and an internet connection, Belle delved into the world of online entrepreneurship. She recognized the potential of e-commerce and decided to start her own online boutique, specializing in handmade jewelry and accessories. It was a leap of faith, and the path was fraught with challenges, but Belle was undeterred.

She poured her heart and soul into her online store, designing unique pieces and leveraging social media to showcase her creations. Late nights turned into early mornings as she juggled her online business with her day job, determined to make her venture a success.

Belle's breakthrough came when she decided to share her journey on social media. She documented the highs and lows of entrepreneurship, offering glimpses into the process of creating her jewelry and the dedication required to build a brand. Her authenticity resonated with her growing audience, and her online following began to swell.

As her online boutique gained traction, Belle seized the opportunity to expand her horizons. She used her platform to advocate for financial literacy and entrepreneurship among young women, inspiring them to pursue their passions and achieve financial independence. Belle's call to action was simple yet powerful: "Are you ready to transform your life?"

Her message struck a chord with her followers, many of whom started their own businesses and pursued their dreams. Belle's impact extended beyond her online store; she became a mentor and a source of inspiration for aspiring entrepreneurs.

One of Belle's mentees, Emily, took her advice to heart and started her own online business. With Belle's guidance, Emily's venture flourished, and she went on to become a successful e-commerce entrepreneur. Belle's influence had a ripple effect, creating a community of empowered women who were charting their paths to success.

Mr. Grant Money had the privilege of meeting Belle during a conference on entrepreneurship. Her story left a profound impression, showcasing the power of determination, authenticity, and mentorship in achieving success. Belle's journey from a small-town dreamer to a successful online entrepreneur and mentor was a testament to the transformative power of passion and perseverance.

In his Golden Journal, Mr. Grant Money penned a quote inspired by Belle's story: "Success is not a destination but a journey fueled by passion, authenticity, and the desire to empower others along the way." Belle's call to action had ignited a spark of transformation in the lives of many, proving that with the right mindset, anyone could transform their life and achieve their dreams.

Adrian Turner's Tech Treasures: Coding Dreams, Unlocking Futures

Adrian Turner's Inspiring Tale Of Turning Code Into Scholarships, Dreams, And A Brighter Future

In the heart of Dallas, where the skyline gleamed with modernity, Mr. Grant Money discovered the inspiring story of Adrian Turner, a high school student with a passion for technology and a vision for change. Dressed in a hoodie adorned with coding symbols, Adrian was not just another student but a tech trailblazer.

Adrian Turner's journey began in the bustling halls of Dallas High School, where he recognized the untapped potential of students eager to explore the world of technology. He envisioned a scholarship program that supported academic pursuits and encouraged creative problem-solving in the digital realm.

Adrian Turner's "Tech Treasures" initiative took shape as a series of coding workshops held at the school's state-of-the-art computer lab. With a knack for simplifying complex concepts, Adrian guided his peers through the intricacies of coding languages, turning the once-intimidating world of technology into an exciting treasure hunt.

Adrian Turner ingeniously transformed the workshops into interactive coding competitions to fund the Tech Treasures Scholarship. Participants paid a nominal fee to join, and the winners received not only the admiration of their peers but also the satisfaction of contributing to the scholarship fund.

The coding competitions were more than just learning experiences; they became a community event, attracting local tech enthusiasts, mentors, and even representatives from tech companies. Adrian Turner's vision extended beyond the confines of the school, creating a network of support for students with a passion for technology.

As the Tech Treasures Scholarship fund grew, Adrian Turner sought partnerships with tech companies willing to invest in the next generation of innovators. His persuasive pitch and the success stories of scholarship recipients convinced local businesses that supporting Tech Treasures was an investment in the future of technology.

One scholarship recipient, Maria Chavez, dreamt of developing accessible technology for individuals with disabilities. With the Tech Treasures Scholarship's support, Maria pursued a computer science degree specializing in assistive technology. Her groundbreaking projects caught the attention of both local and national tech organizations, propelling her to the forefront of innovation.

News of Adrian Turner's Tech Treasures reached Mr. Grant Money, who couldn't resist the call of Dallas to witness the impact firsthand. The coding workshop he attended buzzed with energy as students collaborated, problem-solved, and envisioned a future where technology was a tool for positive change.

Adrian Turner welcomed Mr. Grant Money, proudly showcasing the Tech Treasures Scholarship recipients and the innovative projects born from the coding competitions. The atmosphere resonated with the spirit of collaboration, creativity, and a shared vision for a tech-savvy future.

As Mr. Grant Money departed Dallas, he carried with him the story of Adrian Turner—a symbol of how a student's passion, coupled with innovative thinking, could open doors to education and opportunity. The Tech Treasures Scholarship was not merely a financial aid program; it was a testament to the transformative power of technology in the hands of the next generation.

In his Golden Journal, Mr. Grant Money penned a quote inspired by Adrian Turner's story: "In the digital realm, every line of code is a key unlocking the doors to education, creativity, and a future where technology becomes a force for positive change."

Exercise: "Innovate for Impact: Scholarship Fundraising Challenge"

Objective: This exercise empowers youth to brainstorm and create a fundraising plan to generate $10,000 for ten $1,000 scholarships for deserving students at their high school.

Materials Needed:
- Large sheets of paper or poster boards
- Markers, pens, and colored pencils
- Sticky notes
- Flip chart or whiteboard and markers

Instructions:

1. Introduction (10 minutes):
- Share the story of Adrian Turner's Tech Treasures briefly to inspire participants with the concept of student-led scholarship creation.
- Explain the challenge: to raise $10,000 to fund ten $1,000 scholarships for deserving students at their high school.

2. Brainstorming Session (20 minutes):
- Facilitate a group brainstorming session where participants generate ideas for fundraising. Encourage creativity and remind them that the goal is not only to raise funds but also to create a positive impact.

3. Idea Sorting (15 minutes):
- Have participants write each fundraising idea on a sticky note.
- Create a visual display on a whiteboard or flip chart where participants can place their sticky notes, sorting ideas into categories such as events, partnerships, online campaigns, and community involvement.

4. Building the Plan (30 minutes):
- Divide participants into small groups.
- Instruct each group to choose one or more fundraising ideas from the display and build a comprehensive plan. They should consider logistics, budget, timeline, and potential community engagement.

5. Group Presentations (30 minutes):
- Each group presents their fundraising plan to the entire group.
- Emphasize the need for creativity, feasibility, and community involvement in their proposals.

6. Feedback and Collaboration (20 minutes):
- After each presentation, encourage feedback and suggestions from the rest of the participants.
- Encourage collaboration between groups to enhance and refine ideas.

7. Selection of Winning Plan (15 minutes):
- Collectively discuss the strengths and weaknesses of each plan.
- Facilitate a group decision to select the most promising fundraising plan based on impact, feasibility, and creativity.

8. Action Steps and Commitment (20 minutes):
- Instruct participants to outline specific action steps for implementing the chosen fundraising plan.
- Encourage a commitment from each participant to actively contribute to the execution of the plan.

9. Reflection and Journaling (15 minutes):
- Provide time for individual reflection and journaling. Participants can write down their thoughts on the exercise, what they learned, and their personal commitment to making a difference.

10. Closing Thoughts (10 minutes):
- Conclude the exercise by summarizing key takeaways and expressing enthusiasm for the impact they can collectively create.
- Encourage participants to stay engaged and motivated throughout the fundraising process.

This "Innovate for Impact" exercise engages participants in creative thinking and encourages teamwork, problem-solving, and community involvement. It empowers youth to take ownership of a meaningful initiative, fostering a sense of responsibility and leadership in scholarship creation.

Discussion Questions

1. How did Adrian Turner's Tech Treasures initiative successfully bridge the gap between the high school environment and the broader tech community, creating a network of support for students passionate about technology?

2. The coding competitions not only served as learning experiences but also contributed to the Tech Treasures Scholarship fund. What impact did this innovative funding model have on the program's sustainability and ability to support students like Maria Chavez?

3. Adrian Turner's vision extended beyond traditional education, involving partnerships with local tech companies. How did these partnerships contribute to the success of the Tech Treasures Scholarship, and what role did they play in fostering a collaborative environment for students?

4. Maria Chavez's story highlights the transformative power of the Tech Treasures Scholarship. How can initiatives like these inspire and empower students to pursue innovative projects that address real-world challenges, as seen in Maria's work in assistive technology?

5. Mr. Grant Money's quote, "In the digital realm, every line of code is a key unlocking the doors to education, creativity, and a future where technology becomes a force for positive change," encapsulates the essence of Adrian Turner's story. How can this philosophy be applied more broadly to education and technology initiatives to create positive change in communities beyond Dallas?

 Big Idea "Innovate for Accessibility Challenge"

Inspired by Maria Chavez's journey, students and teachers could organize an "Innovate for Accessibility Challenge" at their school. This challenge would encourage students to develop technology solutions that enhance accessibility for individuals with disabilities. Participants would engage in coding workshops focused on assistive technology, and the challenge would provide a platform for students to apply their skills in creating meaningful, real-world solutions. Local disability advocacy groups, organizations, and experts could be invited to judge the projects. The winning solutions could be further developed or implemented in collaboration with relevant stakeholders, turning the competition into a catalyst for positive impact in the community..

🔍 Word Search

Welcome to the "Mr. Grant Money Wordsearch Puzzle," where we dive into the inspirational story of Adrian Turner, a high school tech trailblazer from the heart of Dallas. As we explore the transformative power of technology and education

Discover the words hidden in this puzzle that capture the essence of Adrian's journey and the Tech Treasures Scholarship initiative. Join us on this word hunt, and unlock the coding treasures that pave the way for a brighter future!

Now, here are the 14 words for the word search puzzle based on the story:

C	O	L	L	A	B	O	R	A	T	I	O	N	R
Y	T	D	L	E	Y	T	I	N	U	M	M	O	C
T	I	T	A	T	U	R	N	E	R	I	S	O	N
I	S	A	L	L	A	D	R	N	A	I	C	O	G
V	M	O	Y	G	O	L	O	N	H	C	E	T	I
I	O	N	C	O	D	I	N	G	M	C	F	N	E
T	R	A	N	S	F	O	R	M	A	T	I	V	E
A	O	I	A	N	I	O	C	E	I	I	R	H	R
E	B	P	I	H	S	R	A	L	O	H	C	S	L
R	T	I	R	T	G	D	O	N	N	N	T	Y	C
C	R	N	D	T	S	R	O	T	N	E	M	O	H
O	Y	N	A	I	O	P	O	H	S	K	R	O	W
A	I	N	N	O	V	A	T	I	O	N	R	O	A
O	P	P	O	R	T	U	N	I	T	Y	A	T	N

COMMUNITY
TRANSFORMATIVE
INNOVATION
ADRIAN
DALLAS
COLLABORATION
TURNER
CREATIVITY
OPPORTUNITY
CODING
WORKSHOP
TECHNOLOGY
SCHOLARSHIP
MENTORS

"In the heart of every community, there lies untapped potential, and in the halls of every school, there are visionaries waiting to emerge. Adrian Turner's Tech Treasures Scholarship teaches us that with passion, innovation, and a collaborative spirit, we can turn a simple idea into a transformative force."

SUCCESS STORIES

"Resilience Rewritten: From Failure to Finance Trailblazer – Janice's Inspirational Journey"

"Let me tell you about the time I failed miserably," Janice began with a chuckle, drawing the attention of her eager audience. Dressed in professional attire, she radiated confidence and positivity as she embarked on a journey of resilience and triumph.

Janice's tale unfolded in the bustling city of Chicago, a place known for its towering skyscrapers and indomitable spirit. In the world of finance, where numbers often dictated success, Janice was determined to carve her own path.

Fresh out of college, armed with a degree in finance and a heart full of ambition, Janice secured her first job at a prestigious investment firm. She had high hopes and envisioned a flourishing career in the financial world. However, reality had other plans in store for her.

Her early days at the firm were challenging, to say the least. The complex algorithms, fast-paced trading, and high-stakes decisions left her feeling overwhelmed. It seemed like every attempt she made was met with failure, and Janice began to doubt her abilities.

But instead of succumbing to self-doubt, Janice decided to embrace her failures as stepping stones to success. She sought guidance from her mentors, learned from her mistakes, and dedicated herself to continuous improvement.

One day, Janice stumbled upon an opportunity to work on a groundbreaking project—an algorithm that aimed to revolutionize the firm's trading strategies. It was a daunting task, but Janice saw it as a chance to prove herself.

With unwavering determination, she poured her heart and soul into the project. Late nights at the office became her norm as she meticulously fine-tuned the algorithm. Despite facing setbacks and encountering obstacles, Janice remained resilient.

Months of hard work and perseverance paid off when the algorithm not only met but exceeded expectations. It was a game-changer for the firm, garnering attention and praise from colleagues and superiors alike. Janice's journey from initial failure to this remarkable achievement was nothing short of inspiring.

As she concluded her story, Janice left her audience with a powerful message: "Failure is not the end; it's an opportunity to learn, grow, and eventually succeed. Embrace your setbacks, stay resilient, and keep moving forward. The path to success is often paved with the lessons learned from failure."

Janice's story served as a reminder that setbacks and challenges are an integral part of any success story. Her transformation from a struggling novice to a finance trailblazer inspired others to persevere in the face of adversity and use failures as stepping stones to reach their goals.

BEYOND THE VEIL

The Amazing Adventures of
MR GRANT MONEY

Beyond the Veil: Mr. Grant Money's Odyssey in the Pool of Reflection

Unveiling The Mystical Tapestry Of Scholarships, Education, And The Ripple Effect Of Positive Change

In the quiet hours of an enchanting evening, Mr. Grant Money found himself wandering through a realm that existed somewhere between dreams and reality. The moon hung low in the indigo sky, casting a gentle glow on the path that stretched before him. As he ambled along, a soft voice carried on the breeze—a whisper from Jerla, his angelic guide.

"Mr. Grant Money," she said, "come closer. There is a place I wish to show you."

Following the ethereal melody of Jerla's voice, Mr. Grant Money found himself standing before a pool unlike any other. Its surface shimmered with a mesmerizing light, reflecting the myriad possibilities that danced in the air. Jerla explained this was the Pool of Reflection—a sacred place where the wisdom of the past and the potential of the future converged.

As Mr. Grant Money gazed into the pool, images of students embarking on educational journeys unfolded before him. Each ripple in the water told a story—a tale of triumph, resilience, and the transformative power of education.

"Step into the pool," urged Jerla. "Let the reflections guide you."

With anticipation, Mr. Grant Money stepped into the pool, feeling a gentle warmth enveloping him. Instead of wetness, the water carried the weight of knowledge and experience.

Instantly, the pool began to reveal scenes from the lives of scholarship recipients—students who had navigated challenges, pursued their passions and forged new paths. Mr. Grant Money witnessed moments of joy as acceptance letters arrived, tears of perseverance in the face of adversity, and the profound impact scholarships had on shaping destinies.

As the scenes unfolded, Jerla explained, "Every scholarship creates ripples of knowledge, empowerment, and positive change. These ripples extend far beyond the individual, touching the lives of families, communities, and the world."

Mr. Grant Money marveled at the interconnected web of scholarship impacts, where a single act of generosity could set in motion a cascade of opportunities for countless others.

With each step in the pool, Mr. Grant Money absorbed the lessons embedded in the reflections. He learned about the importance of fostering a love for learning, providing support to those in need, and creating a culture where education became a beacon of hope.

As the visions ended, Jerla said, "Mr. Grant Money, carry the wisdom of the Pool of Reflection into the world. Let it be a reminder that education and scholarships are not just pathways to personal success but bridges that connect individuals and communities in a tapestry of shared aspirations."

With newfound clarity, Mr. Grant Money emerged from the Pool of Reflection, his mind buzzing with inspiration. He knew that the stories he had witnessed would become the foundation of his mission—to empower students, create ripples of positive change, and inspire a world where education was a beacon for all.

Armed with the insights from the mystical pool, Mr. Grant Money set forth on a renewed journey. The stories from the Pool of Reflection became the heart of his advocacy, echoing in the pages of his books, the halls of schools, and the hearts of those who aspired to make a difference.

As the moon bathed the realm in its serene glow, Jerla's voice lingered, "Continue to be the bearer of scholarship wisdom, Mr. Grant Money. The Pool of Reflection will always guide those seeking education's transformative power."

And so, with a heart full of purpose, Mr. Grant Money ventured back into the world, ready to share the profound lessons learned from the Pool of Reflection and continue his quest to make education and scholarships a transformative force for all.

"In the shimmering waters of the Pool of Reflection, I discovered that a scholarship is not just a financial aid—it's a ripple that transforms lives, creating a symphony of opportunities that echoes through generations."

- Mr. Grant Money

Exercise: "Reflect and Inspire"

Objective: This exercise aims to encourage participants to reflect on their educational journey, identify the transformative moments, and create an inspirational message or artwork that represents the impact of education and scholarships.

Materials Needed:
- Journals or sheets of paper
- Pens, pencils, markers, or colored pencils
- Large sheets of paper or a whiteboard
- Art supplies (optional)

Instructions:

1. Personal Reflection (15 minutes):
- Ask participants to find a quiet space and reflect on their educational journey. Encourage them to consider the pivotal moments, challenges overcome, and the role education has played in shaping their lives.

2. Pool of Reflection Visualization (10 minutes):
- Guide participants through a brief visualization exercise. Ask them to close their eyes and imagine standing before a mystical Pool of Reflection. In this pool, they see reflections of significant educational moments. Encourage them to explore the details of these reflections.

3. Written Reflection (20 minutes):
- Instruct participants to write down their reflections on paper. They can focus on specific scholarship experiences, transformative educational moments, or the impact of education on their personal and professional development.

4. Artistic Expression (30 minutes - Optional):
- For those who enjoy artistic expression, provide art supplies and encourage them to create visual representations of their reflections. This could include drawings, paintings, or collages that capture the essence of their educational journey.

5. Sharing Circle (20 minutes):
- Form a sharing circle where participants have the option to share their written reflections or showcase their artistic creations. This provides an opportunity for individuals to express the unique aspects of their educational journeys.

6. Reflective Quotes (15 minutes):

- Ask participants to distill the essence of their reflections into short, impactful quotes. These quotes should encapsulate the transformative power of education and scholarships in their lives.

7. Create a Collaborative Mural (30 minutes - Optional):

- If space allows, create a collaborative mural using the quotes and artistic creations. Each participant can contribute a piece, forming a collective representation of the diverse impact of education.

8. Closing Discussion (15 minutes):

- Facilitate a discussion on the collective reflections and inspirations shared during the exercise. Encourage participants to express how their experiences align with the broader themes of the transformative power of education.

9. Setting Intentions (10 minutes):

- Conclude the exercise by asking participants to set intentions for how they can pay forward the impact of education and scholarships. How can they contribute to the educational journeys of others?

This "Reflect and Inspire" exercise provides a meaningful opportunity for participants to delve into their educational experiences, share insights, and collectively celebrate the transformative power of education and scholarships in their lives.

> "As I stepped into the Pool of Reflection, I felt the weight of knowledge replacing the water around me. It taught me that education isn't just a journey—it's a shared odyssey where every scholarship sets in motion a current of positive change, binding us all in a tapestry of aspirations."
>
> - Mr. Grant Money

Discussion Questions

1. What symbolic elements in the story represent the transformative power of education, and how do they contribute to the overall message of the narrative?

2. Discuss the significance of the Pool of Reflection as a metaphor for the impact of scholarships. How does the imagery of the pool convey the interconnectedness of educational opportunities and their far-reaching effects?

3. In the story, Mr. Grant Money learns important lessons about the role of education as a bridge connecting individuals and communities. How can these lessons be applied to real-world initiatives or policies aimed at promoting education and scholarship opportunities?

4. Explore the role of Jerla as an angelic guide in the narrative. What does her character symbolize, and how does her guidance contribute to the story's exploration of the deeper meaning of scholarships and education?

5. Reflect on the idea of "ripples of knowledge, empowerment, and positive change" created by scholarships, as mentioned by Jerla. How can individuals, communities, and societies work together to amplify and sustain these ripples for long-term impact?

 Big Idea "Ripple of Inspiration Workshops"

Inspired by the interconnected web of scholarship impacts witnessed in the Pool of Reflection, teachers and students can collaborate to create "Ripple of Inspiration Workshops" within their schools or communities. These workshops would serve as platforms for scholarship recipients to share their personal stories, struggles, and triumphs. Through presentations, discussions, and interactive activities, students can learn firsthand about the transformative power of education. Additionally, these workshops could involve successful professionals who once benefited from scholarships, reinforcing the idea that education is a lifelong journey. By organizing and participating in these workshops, students not only gain valuable insights but also contribute to building a supportive and inspiring educational culture within their community.

🔍 Word Search

Embark on a captivating journey with Mr. Grant Money as he explores the mystical realm between dreams and reality. In the enchanting glow of an indigo sky, guided by the ethereal voice of Jerla, he discovers the extraordinary Pool of Reflection.

Join Mr. Grant Money as he steps into the pool, absorbing the wisdom that creates ripples of knowledge, empowerment, and positive change. The Puzzle that follows captures the essence of this extraordinary adventure.

Now, here are the 15 words for the word search puzzle based on the story:

A	R	I	N	S	P	I	R	A	T	I	O	N	P
D	I	T	R	O	C	O	G	O	A	I	D	S	O
V	P	I	B	E	A	C	O	N	I	L	O	T	C
O	P	V	I	O	T	O	T	E	A	O	O	C	N
C	L	S	N	G	E	N	E	R	O	S	I	T	Y
A	E	D	U	C	A	T	I	O	N	O	I	G	I
C	I	L	R	E	S	I	L	I	E	N	C	E	D
Y	Y	R	T	S	E	P	A	T	T	S	S	E	E
E	A	S	P	I	R	A	T	I	O	N	M	E	S
Y	S	P	I	E	S	O	O	E	Q	U	E	S	T
R	E	F	L	E	C	T	I	O	N	A	T	O	I
P	S	C	H	O	L	A	R	S	H	I	P	D	N
T	E	M	P	O	W	E	R	M	E	N	T	I	Y
T	R	A	N	S	F	O	R	M	A	T	I	V	E

REFLECTION
DESTINY
RESILIENCE
ADVOCACY
INSPIRATION
BEACON
TRANSFORMATIVE
QUEST
GENEROSITY
RIPPLE
EMPOWERMENT
EDUCATION
TAPESTRY
ASPIRATION
SCHOLARSHIP

"In the enchanted realm between dreams and reality, where the Pool of Reflection reveals the interconnected stories of resilience and triumph, we learn that education, like the moon's glow, is a universal beacon guiding us towards a world where every individual's pursuit of knowledge creates a ripple effect of empowerment for all."

SUCCESS STORIES

"From Adversity to Triumph: Arianne's Inspiring Journey Fueled by Scholarships and Determination"

"We've all faced setbacks in life," Arianne began, her voice steady and unwavering as she stood before a captivated audience. Dressed in a simple yet elegant attire, she radiated resilience. Her journey from adversity to triumph had the room hanging onto her every word.

Arianne's story began in a small town where opportunities were scarce, and dreams often seemed out of reach. Despite the challenges, she was determined to pursue her passion for education. However, life had a different plan for her when a sudden family crisis forced her to put her dreams on hold.

In the face of adversity, Arianne did not yield. Instead, she used the setback as a springboard for her future. She started working odd jobs, saving every penny, and enrolling in evening classes to continue her education. Arianne's determination to overcome obstacles became her driving force.

During this time, Arianne stumbled upon a local scholarship opportunity. With a heart full of hope, she applied, pouring her dreams and aspirations into her application essay. Her heartfelt words caught the attention of the scholarship committee, and to her astonishment, she was awarded the scholarship.

The financial support not only relieved Arianne's financial burden but also rekindled her belief in the power of education. With renewed vigor, she completed her degree, excelling in her studies, and went on to pursue a career in education. Arianne became a beacon of hope for her community, inspiring others to overcome adversity and pursue their dreams.

As Arianne concluded her speech, the audience erupted in applause. Her story of resilience and triumph was a testament to the transformative power of scholarships. She had not only overcome setbacks but had also become a source of inspiration for those facing similar challenges.

Arianne's message was clear: setbacks may slow us down, but they do not define us. With determination, resilience, and the support of scholarships, anyone could overcome adversity and achieve their dreams. Her journey from adversity to triumph was a testament to the indomitable human spirit.

In his Golden Journal, Mr. Grant Money captured Arianne's story with a quote that resonated deeply: "In the face of setbacks, scholarships become the stepping stones to triumph, reminding us that our dreams are never out of reach." Arianne's story continued to inspire generations, proving that with perseverance and the support of scholarships, individuals could transform their lives and reach their fullest potential.

CEREMONY OF IMPACT

The Amazing Adventures of
MRGRANTMONEY

Ceremony of Impact: Mr. Grant Money's Scholar S.H.I.P Wisdom

Embark On A Transformative Journey With The Scholarship Sage As He Unveils The Secrets To Navigating The Seas Of Life With Purpose

Amidst the electrifying atmosphere of the grand high school commencement ceremony at Hillcrest High School, over two thousand students clad in their graduation regalia eagerly awaited the momentous occasion. The stadium buzzed with excitement—families and friends packed the stands, the school band played spirited tunes, cheerleaders ignited the crowd, and the air was charged with anticipation.

As the ceremony reached its pinnacle, the principal took the stage, his voice echoing through the stadium, "Ladies and gentlemen, esteemed guests, and the incredible graduating class of Hillcrest High School, it is my honor to introduce a speaker whose impact on our students has been nothing short of extraordinary."

A hush fell over the crowd as the principal continued, "But before I bring him to the stage, let's hear from someone whose life has been tremendously impacted by the wisdom and guidance of our esteemed speaker. Please welcome Jason Strong!"

Applause erupted as Jason, a shining example of Mr. Grant Money's influence, stepped forward. With sincerity in his voice, Jason shared heartfelt words about the Scholarship Sage, describing him as a beacon of inspiration and a catalyst for positive change. The cheers swelled as many in the audience recognized the impact of Mr. Grant Money's insights, with numerous students having secured scholarships of various amounts.

As the DJ cued the "Scholarship Sage" song, Mr. Grant Money made his way to the microphone, greeted by thunderous applause. Dapperly dressed, he exuded an air of wisdom and charisma as he began to address the vast assembly of students, families, and friends.

"Good evening, graduates! What an incredible journey it has been, and an honor to stand before a sea of potential, determination, and dreams!" Mr. Grant Money's voice carried through the stadium, commanding attention.

He delved into his message, centering it around the concept of Scholar S.H.I.P—Sailing High In Purpose. With eloquence and passion, he imparted five key points to guide the graduates on their journey through life, encouraging them to set sail with purpose, resilience, and a commitment to positive impact.

The 5 Key Points:

1. Navigate with Purpose: "Chart your course with a clear purpose. Know where you want to go, and let your passion be your compass."

2. Embrace the Winds of Change: "Life's winds may not always blow in your favor. Embrace challenges as opportunities to learn and grow, adjusting your sails as needed."

3. Anchors Away from Negativity: "Shed the anchors of negativity that may weigh you down. Surround yourself with positivity and those who uplift you."

4. Celebrate the Small Victories: "Every journey is made up of small victories. Celebrate them, for they are the building blocks of your success."

5. Pass the Compassion Torch: "As you sail high in purpose, extend a hand to those around you. The ripple effect of kindness can change lives and communities."

"Remember, graduates, a commencement is not an ending but a beginning," Mr. Grant Money proclaimed, his words resonating through the hearts of the graduating class. The stadium erupted in applause and cheers, the energy reaching a crescendo as Mr. Grant Money concluded his powerful address.

"In the vast sea of life, be the captains of your destinies, sail high in purpose, and let your ripples of positive impact transform the world around you. Congratulations, Hillcrest High School graduates!"

With those words, Mr. Grant Money left the stage, leaving behind a wave of inspiration that reverberated through the stadium. The commencement ended not with a mere ceremony but with a ruckus celebration, marking the beginning of a new chapter for each graduate.

As families cheered, friends embraced, and the echoes of celebration filled the air, Mr. Grant Money's impactful message lingered—a guiding light for the graduates as they set sail on their journeys, ready to make waves of positive change in the world.

"In the grand ocean of opportunities, let the winds of purpose fill your sails. Chart your course with passion as your compass, and you'll navigate the waves of life, Sailing High In Purpose!"

- Mr. Grant Money

Exercise: "Set Sail with Purpose"

Objective: This exercise encourages participants to reflect on their goals and aspirations, chart a course for their future, and develop a plan to navigate challenges while positively impacting their communities.

Materials Needed:
- Paper or journals
- Pens or pencils
- Markers or colored pencils
- Large sheets of paper or a whiteboard

Instructions:

1. Reflection (15 minutes):
- Ask participants to find a quiet space and reflect on their personal goals and aspirations. What do they want to achieve in the next five years? Encourage them to write down their thoughts in their journals.

2. Chart Your Course (20 minutes):
- Instruct participants to draw a symbolic representation of their personal journey on a large sheet of paper or a whiteboard. This could include visual elements such as a ship, waves, and destinations representing their goals.

3. Identify Challenges (15 minutes):
- Have participants list potential challenges or obstacles they might encounter on their journey. Emphasize both personal and external challenges that could impact their goals.

4. Develop Strategies (20 minutes):
- Encourage participants to brainstorm strategies for overcoming the challenges they identified. These strategies could include seeking support, building resilience, and staying focused on their goals.

5. Positive Anchors (15 minutes):
- Ask participants to identify positive influences and support systems in their lives. These could be friends, family, mentors, or personal strengths that will anchor them during challenging times.

6. Create a Compassionate Ripple (20 minutes):

- Discuss the concept of the ripple effect and how small acts of kindness can make a big impact. Have participants brainstorm ways they can contribute positively to their communities, creating ripples of kindness.

7. Share and Discuss (30 minutes):

- Create a safe and open space for participants to share their symbolic representations, challenges, strategies, positive anchors, and ideas for creating a compassionate ripple.
- Facilitate a group discussion to encourage collaboration, sharing of insights, and support among participants.

8. Action Plan (15 minutes):

- Instruct participants to develop a personal action plan based on their reflections and the group discussion. This plan should outline specific steps they will take to navigate challenges, stay focused on their goals, and contribute positively to their communities.

9. Gallery Walk (15 minutes):

- Allow participants to showcase their symbolic representations and action plans in a gallery walk format. This provides an opportunity for everyone to gain inspiration from each other's journeys.

10. Closing Reflection (10 minutes):

- Conclude the exercise with a brief reflection on the importance of setting sail with purpose, navigating challenges, and creating positive ripples in their communities. Encourage participants to carry these lessons into their future endeavors.

This "Set Sail with Purpose" activity combines self-reflection, goal-setting, and community impact, aligning with the themes of Mr. Grant Money's Commencement Address.

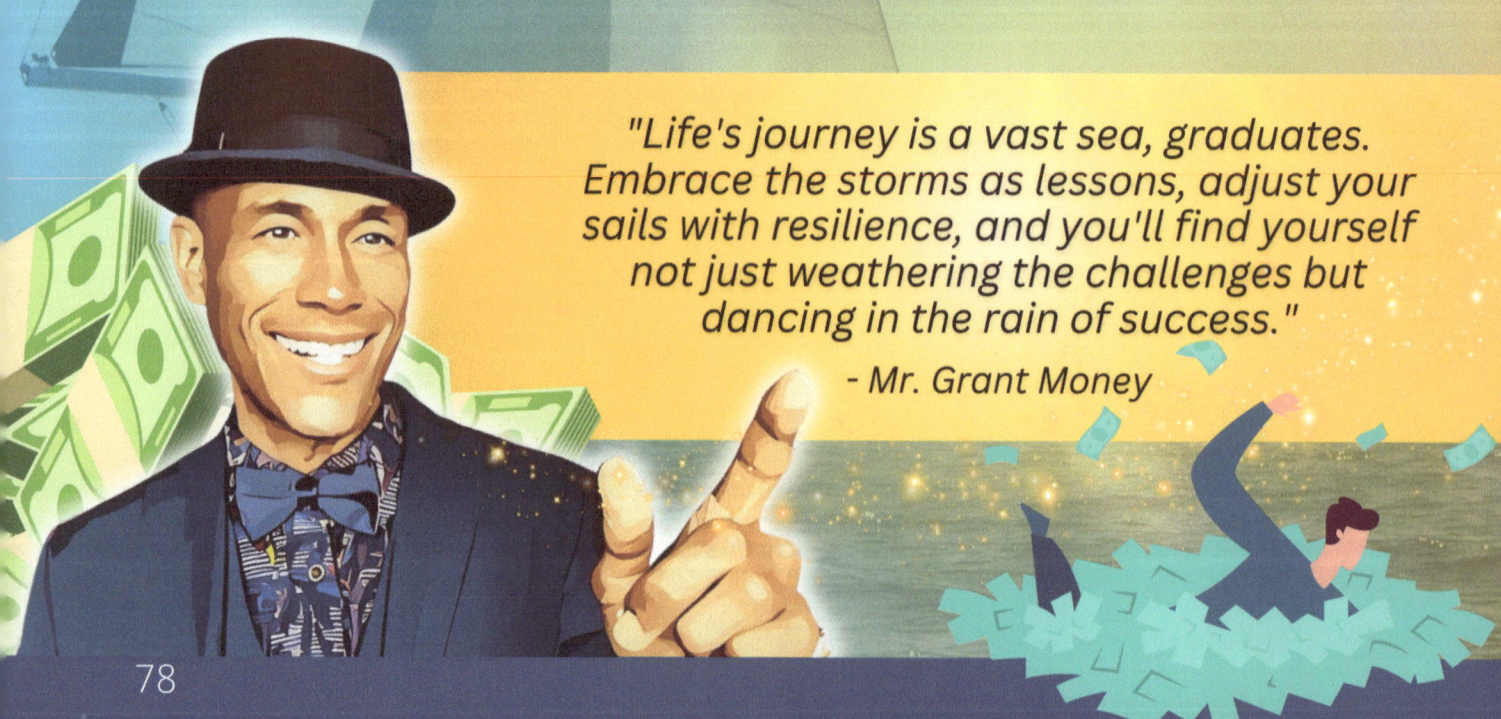

"Life's journey is a vast sea, graduates. Embrace the storms as lessons, adjust your sails with resilience, and you'll find yourself not just weathering the challenges but dancing in the rain of success."

- Mr. Grant Money

Discussion Questions

1. Mr. Grant Money emphasized the importance of navigating life with a clear purpose. How has the idea of purpose played a role in your own life so far, and how do you envision it guiding your future decisions and actions?

2. The Scholarship Sage encourages graduates to embrace life's challenges as opportunities for growth. Can you share a personal experience where facing a challenge led to personal or academic growth? How did it shape your perspective on overcoming obstacles?

3. Mr. Grant Money advised shedding the anchors of negativity and surrounding oneself with positivity. In your opinion, how can individuals proactively create a positive environment for themselves and others, especially in the face of challenges and uncertainties?

4. The idea of celebrating small victories is a key point in Mr. Grant Money's message. Reflecting on your academic journey or personal achievements, what are some small victories that you've encountered, and how have they contributed to your overall sense of accomplishment?

5. Mr. Grant Money emphasized the importance of extending a hand to others and the ripple effect of kindness. How can graduates actively incorporate compassion into their lives and communities, and what role do you think small acts of kindness play in creating positive change on a larger scale?

💡 **Big Idea** "Scholar S.H.I.P. Journaling Program"

Encourage students to create and maintain personal journals inspired by Mr. Grant Money's key points. Teachers can introduce journaling prompts aligned with each principle, guiding students to reflect on their goals, challenges, victories, and acts of compassion. The journaling program not only enhances students' self-awareness and resilience but also provides a tangible record of their growth throughout their academic journey. Periodic sharing sessions or peer reviews can foster a supportive community where students learn from each other's experiences and inspire one another to stay committed to their purposes.

🔍 Word Search

Amid the electrifying atmosphere of the grand high school commencement ceremony at Hillcrest High School, the Scholarship Sage, Mr. Grant Money, left an indelible mark on the graduating class.

In celebration of this momentous occasion, we present the "Mr. Grant Money Wordsearch Puzzle," featuring the words related to the inspiring wisdom shared by the Scholarship Sage.

Now, here are the 15 words for the word search puzzle based on the story:

```
H L C E L E B R A T E I G O
N I R O I I E W I A N N O S
B E S C I R M L Y P S T L C
C O M P A S S P W S R N I N
E N D I G D O V A R E E R E
C E S O P R U P O C G M R G
N C I G N I L I A S T E S A
E C P I H S R A L O H C S T
I I J O U R N E Y I E N G I
L P O S I T I V E O G E N V
I N S P I R A T I O N M S I
S K N O W L E D G E C M Y T
E Y G U I D A N C E U O E Y
R V I C T O R I E S C C I C
```

PURPOSE
COMMENCEMENT
IMPACT
NEGATIVITY
GUIDANCE
SCHOLARSHIP
POSITIVE
RESILIENCE
VICTORIES
JOURNEY
COMPASS
INSPIRATION
KNOWLEDGE
CELEBRATE
SAILING

MR. GRANT MONEY

"In the symphony of life, let your melody be one of purpose and positivity. Celebrate the small victories, for they compose the beautiful score of your success, echoing through the chapters of your journey."

SUCCESS STORIES

"From Garage to Global Impact: Hopie Rodriguez's Inspiring Journey in Saving the World"

The world was on the brink of disaster until Hope "Hopie" Rodriguez emerged as an unexpected savior. In the midst of a global crisis, where adversity loomed like a relentless storm, Hopie, a young scientist, discovered a groundbreaking solution that not only averted catastrophe but also set her on a path to extraordinary success.

Born with an insatiable curiosity and a passion for science, Hopie had always been a seeker of knowledge. Her journey began in the humble surroundings of her family's garage, which doubled as her makeshift laboratory. Despite limited resources, she conducted experiments, nurtured her love for chemistry, and dreamed of a future where her discoveries could change the world.

However, the world had different plans for Hopie when a global environmental crisis struck. A series of devastating events threatened ecosystems, agriculture, and human survival. The situation seemed dire, and scientists worldwide were struggling to find a solution.

In a moment of clarity, Hopie remembered her garage experiments, where she had dabbled in soil chemistry and sustainable agriculture. Armed with determination and an unshakable belief that science held the answers, she embarked on a mission to develop an innovative, eco-friendly soil treatment that could rejuvenate barren lands and combat environmental degradation.

Countless sleepless nights and tireless experiments later, Hopie's breakthrough arrived. She had created a revolutionary soil treatment that not only restored fertility to damaged lands but also enhanced crop yields while minimizing environmental harm. Her discovery promised to be a game-changer in the fight against global environmental crises.

With her groundbreaking solution in hand, Hopie sought to share her invention with the world. She reached out to environmental organizations, agricultural experts, and government agencies, eager to contribute to the restoration of damaged ecosystems. The impact was immediate—barren lands began to flourish, and agricultural yields soared, offering hope to communities facing environmental devastation.

Hopie's story became a global sensation, inspiring young scientists and change-makers around the world. She received accolades, invitations to speak at international conferences, and partnerships with organizations dedicated to environmental sustainability. Her invention not only averted disaster but also opened doors to a future where science and innovation held the key to solving some of humanity's most pressing challenges.

In the face of adversity, Hopie had risen to the occasion, proving that determination, innovation, and a passion for positive change could lead to extraordinary success. Her journey from a humble garage laboratory to a global environmental champion became an iconic tale of resilience and inspiration, reminding the world that even in the darkest moments, hope could shine through with the power to transform the future.

AFTERWARD

As you turn the last pages of The Amazing Adventures of Mr. Grant Money, Volume 5, take a moment to reflect on the journey we've traveled together. These stories of bold exploits and transformative opportunities weren't just entertaining—they were packed with lessons for navigating the world of grants and philanthropy.

At its core, this series has shown that success in grant acquisition is within everyone's reach. Each adventure served as a reminder that behind every triumphant proposal is a willingness to learn, adapt, and take action. Whether you're just starting or refining your expertise, the wisdom shared here is a stepping stone for your own achievements.

But knowledge alone isn't the key—action is. Just like Mr. Grant Money, those who succeed in the grant world embrace the courage to move forward, even from ground zero. The lessons from these tales are like treasure maps, pointing the way. The real value lies in taking that journey and putting the strategies into practice.

As this series concludes, the focus shifts to you and your story. What challenges will you conquer? What treasures will you unearth for your community or mission? The possibilities are endless, and now you're equipped to take your next steps with confidence.

If you're eager to expand your skills even further, explore the resources at MrGrantMoney.com and GrantCentralUSA.com. These platforms offer courses, tools, and expert guidance to deepen your expertise and help you transform knowledge into results.

While this is the final chapter of Mr. Grant Money's adventures, it's the opening of a new chapter in your journey. With every insight and strategy you've gained, you're prepared to make a meaningful impact. The world of grants is vast, but so is your potential.

So, as you close this book, open the door to new opportunities. Let the lessons inspire you, the resources guide you, and your own determination lead the way. The adventure doesn't end here—it begins with you.

ABOUT THE AUTHOR

Rodney Walker is a man on a mission. He's dedicated his life to helping others secure funding for their projects and dreams. As the President of Grant Central USA, a grant development training firm internationally known for helping organizations land six-figure and seven-figure grants and shave months off the time it takes to get funded, Rodney has helped clients raise over half a billion dollars in grants!

He's also an author of numerous books, online courses and the founder of two popular grant writing conferences: The Education Grants Conference and First Responders Grants Conference. Grant Central USA has also partnered with several universities, including Regis University, Hawaii University, Oklahoma University, National University, Cal Poly University, and Florida Atlantic University.

Rodney is even the host of four podcasts: Get Funded with Rodney, Grant Writing Today, Grant Business Show, and Schools Winning Grants. He oversees Grant Success Advisors, an elite network of approved licensees who deliver today's leading training in grant development systems.

He has an extensive network of high-level contacts, including his Grant Writers Association group on Linkedin with over 15,000+ members.

Considered a national authority in the grant industry, Grant Central USA's clients have included, The Magic Johnson Foundation, the George W. Bush Foundation, Ben Guillory and Danny Glover of the Robey Theatre Company, Hawaii State Teachers Association, United Way, Habitat for Humanity, and numerous school districts and city governments.

Rodney has produced over 730 videos on grant development on his popular YouTube channel and has taught over 240,000 people how to improve their grant writing efforts. "We have been helping our clients successfully get funded and launch new careers in grant writing since 2006 across the U.S. and worldwide, giving them both the competence and the confidence to win the grants at a high level."

He says his primary specialty is "Getting our clients funded with six-figure and seven-figure grants while helping grant professionals get paid what they are worth!"

In addition to his leadership experience at Grant Central USA, he has years of experience in Business and Professional Development in various sectors. He has been a sought-after expert in grant professional development, coaching, and the law of success.

As a media personality, he has interviewed numerous celebrities, including Snoop Dogg, Heisman Trophy Winners: Reggie Bush, Charles Woodson, Professional Boxer Laila Ali, America's Next Top Model Season 19 Winner: Laura James, NBA Champions: Draymond Green, Matt Barnes, National College Football Champions: Coach Mack Brown, and Vince Young, and countless others.

It's safe to say that Rodney knows his stuff regarding grants and working with champions!

MGM Music to Get You Going 🎷 and 🎶 Keep You Soaring!

Music has the power to make life and learning more joyful. Get ready to have a blast with Mr. Grant Money Music, where every tune is fun, upbeat, and filled with positivity. These story-driven songs not only entertain but also educate and inspire, making your journey both enjoyable and enriching. 🎶

Dive into a symphony of stories and inspiration with Mr. Grant Money Music, where every note is a step toward greater success.

You can enjoy Mr. Grant Money Music on most major streaming platforms, including Spotify, Apple Music, and Amazon Music, bringing inspiration and positivity right to your favorite device. 🎧

Diverse Musical Flavors to Satisfy Every Listening Craving

Topical and Seasonal Themes

Enjoy our themed musical sessions that align with the seasons and current events, offering fresh perspectives and innovative ideas from today's Top Master Grant Acquisition Specialist, Mr. Grant Money!

Experience Our Other Dynamic Series with Mr. Grant Money!

Harvesting Hope:
The Global Odyssey of Mr. Grant Money

Vol. 1

ISBN 978-0-9659275-0-5

The Artful Navigator:
Mr. Grant Money's Chronicles

Vol. 2

ISBN 978-0-9659275-2-9

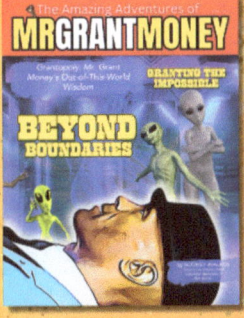

Grantopoly: Mr. Grant Money's Out-of-This-World Wisdom

Vol. 3

ISBN 978-0-9659275-3-6

Grant Odyssey:
Mr. Grant Money's Time-Traveling Feats

Vol. 4

ISBN 978-0-9659275-4-3

Unlocking Powerful Secrets of Grant Acquisition

Vol. 5

ISBN 978-0-9659275-5-0

The Entrepreneurial Classroom: Teens Redefining Success

Vol. 1

ISBN 979-8-89725-005-9

Mindset Mastery:
Developing The Teen Entrepreneurial Spirit

Vol. 2

ISBN 979-8-89725-006-6

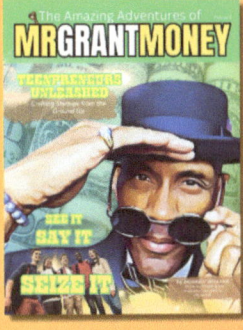

Teenpreneurs Unleashed: Crafting Startups From The Ground Up

Vol. 3

ISBN 979-8-89725-007-3

Business Battlefront: Teens Conquering Challenges In Startups

Vol. 4

ISBN 979-8-89725-008-0

Teen Changemakers: Social Impact Entrepreneurship in Action

Vol. 5

ISBN 979-8-89725-009-7

Pocket Power: A Guide to Practical Budgeting for Teens

Vol. 1

ISBN 979-8-89725-010-3

Fortune Foundations: Navigating Tomorrow's Savings Landscape

Vol. 2

ISBN 979-8-89725-011-0

Profit Pioneers: Young Entrepreneurs Unleashed

Vol. 3

ISBN 979-8-89725-012-7

Scholarly Cents: A College Finance Expedition

Vol. 4

ISBN 979-8-89725-013-4

Financial Fortitude: Navigating Life's Financial Storm

Vol. 5

ISBN 979-8-89725-014-1

Win More Scholarship In Less Time with These...

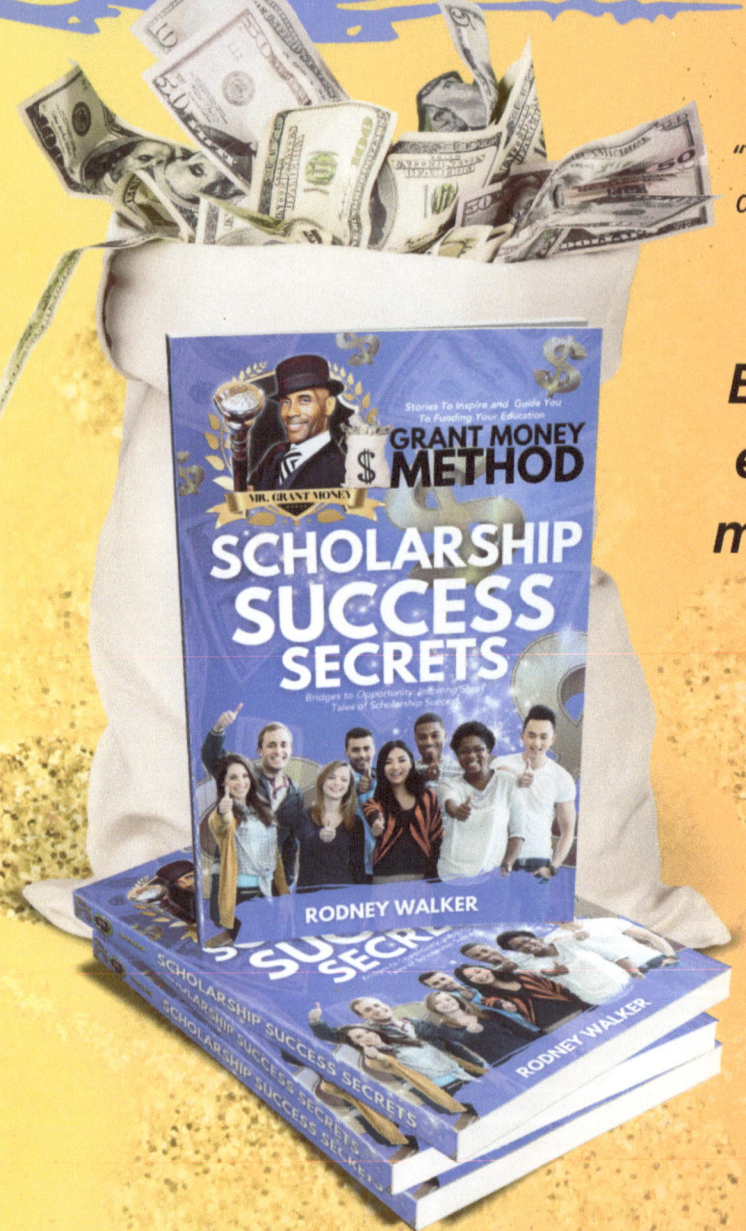

Elevate your scholarship efforts into success with my proven strategies that have raised millions.

Scholarship Success Secret is not just a guide; it's a storytelling journey like no other. Across five compelling books, Mr. Grant Money—takes you into the lives of students, parents, and educators.

Through these vivid, relatable tales, you'll uncover the insider secrets, proven strategies, and practical steps to secure the scholarships and education grants you need for college and beyond.

Boost your confidence in grant writing, fundraising, and finance! Elevate your communication skills with the **Fundraising Fundamentals Vocabulary Builder Series** – *100 essential terms in each series.* Invest in knowledge, empower your success!

Enjoy More Amazing Adventures with Mr. Grant Money!

Scholarship Odyssey:
Mr. Grant Money's Roadmap

Vol. 1

ISBN 979-8-89725-000-4

Journey To Acceptance:
Navigating College Applications

Vol. 2

ISBN 979-8-89725-001-1

Passion Into Practice:
Specialized Scholarship

Vol. 3

ISBN 979-8-89725-002-8

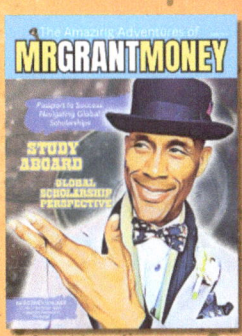
Passport To Success:
Navigating Global Scholarships

Vol. 4

ISBN 979-8-89725-003-5

Empowering Futures:
Scholarships With Lasting Impact

Vol. 5

ISBN 979-8-89725-004-2

Gain Exclusive Access To Companion Resources & Bonus Materials at MrGrantMoney.com and GrantCentralUsa.com

LICENSED

Bring the transformative Adventures and lessons of Mr. Grant Money to your educational institution or organization by **acquiring your license today**. Enjoy exclusive access to a wealth of online resources, such as special reports, worksheets, videos, audio training, discounts, and more, elevating the entire experience to the next level!

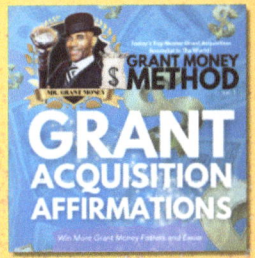

Envision and affirm your grant success in the same proactive spirit as Mr. Grant Money. **Experience the power of these daily affirmations** to inspire and motivate your journey toward success!

www.ingramcontent.com/pod-product-compliance
Lightning Source LLC
Chambersburg PA
CBHW041636050726
47507CB00026B/130